PIERS MORGAN
THE BIOGRAPHY

PIERS MORGAN
THE BIOGRAPHY

Emily Herbert

JOHN BLAKE

Published by John Blake Publishing Ltd,
3 Bramber Court, 2 Bramber Road,
London W14 9PB, England

www.johnblakepublishing.co.uk

www.facebook.com/Johnblakepub facebook
twitter.com/johnblakepub twitter

First published in hardback in 2011

ISBN: 978 1 84358 351 6

British Library Cataloguing-in-Publication Data:

A catalogue record for this book is available from the British Library.

Design by www.envydesign.co.uk

Printed in Great Britain by CPI Mackays, Chatham, ME5 8TD

1 3 5 7 9 10 8 6 4 2

Papers used by John Blake Publishing are natural, recyclable products made from
wood grown in sustainable forests. The manufacturing processes conform to the
environmental regulations of the country of origin.

CONTENTS

CHAPTER ONE
A SUSSEX LAD

The year was 1965, and the Swinging Sixties were well under way: The Beatles and The Rolling Stones were battling it out for the title of Greatest-Ever Rock Band, while society was being turned on its head. Now the age of deference was over and a new egalitarian Britain was born, one that was to replace a keen interest in the lives of the aristocracy with an insatiable appetite for the world of the celebrity. And, on 30 March 1965, a child entered the world who would make a spectacular career on the back of that enthusiasm for celebrity before eventually becoming one himself: Piers Stefan Morgan had arrived. Legend has it that he was named after the brewery heir and privateer motor-racing driver Piers Courage – certainly he would go on to lead a similarly tumultuous life.

Not that he was known as Piers Morgan back then; rather, he was Piers Stefan O'Meara, the first of the two children of Eamon Vincent (a dentist) and Gabrielle

1

O'Meara. His younger brother Jeremy arrived shortly afterwards. 'Vincent', as he was known, would die before his son was one year old. 'When he died, I had a very strong mother and grandmother looking after me, being extra-strong for me and loving me unconditionally,' Piers later recalled. 'My mother has always encouraged her four children [she went on to have two more with her second husband] to live their dreams. If we've ever been in trouble, she's defended us like a lioness.' In fact, Vincent passed away tragically early, at thirty-one; he had been in a car accident and died in the ambulance taking him away from the wreckage.

Piers Morgan's public persona has been a rumbustious one; never afraid of controversy, happy to participate in feuds and always giving as good as he gets. He comes across as extremely brash, something which caused quite a few people to dislike him at one stage in his career, although he calmed down considerably once he made the move from the medium of the printed word to television. Yet there was tragedy in his life from a very early age: to lose a father so young was a terrible sadness. Although he was lucky enough to acquire a stepfather, with whom he became really close, Piers has more in common with the celebrities who tell him about their own problems on ITV's *Piers Morgan's Life Stories* than would at first seem obvious. What's more, he can be far more sympathetic than anyone might expect.

But Piers' relationship with his mother was strong and

this was to see him through the most difficult times until she married for the second time and provided him with a father figure. Although born and brought up in Sussex, he actually has a more international background. Technically, he is one-quarter English, three-quarters Irish (with a little Spanish thrown in): his mother Gabrielle Oliver was born in Battle, Sussex in the 1940s, to Matthew Dudgeon Oliver and Edith Margot Cantopher, who later divorced. Their story is typical of Britain at that time: a life spent in the Colonies, specifically India. Piers' maternal great-grandfather William Joseph Cantopher was born in the province of Deccan in 1891. William's father Bernard was a London University-educated civil engineer, who worked in Berhampore, Murshadibad and Bengal; William later returned to Britain in 1911, where he worked as a stockbroker. He married Edith Mary Kelly, also of Irish descent.

William and Edith had a daughter, Edith Margot, who married Matthew Dudgeon Oliver (who, just to complicate matters, was the son of John Dudgeon Oliver, who was born in China), and it was Matthew, Piers' grandfather, who would go on to work on the *Sunday People* newspaper. Other ancestors have been traced back to Spain and Scotland. Mostly due to this Irish background, the majority of Piers' forebears are Catholic but there is some Presbyterianism in there, too.

When Piers was still a toddler, his artist mother remarried a man with the rather splendid name of

Glynne Pughe-Morgan, from whom he took his surname. The couple went on to have two children, Rupert and Charlotte. Indeed, it was only when he started to make his way as a journalist that Piers dropped the 'Pughe' to make himself seem more egalitarian. In truth, however, his was a privileged background – to begin with, at least.

As an adult, he developed a healthy respect for his brother Jeremy, who went on to serve in the Army (eventually rising to Lieutenant Colonel) but during their childhood the two battled constantly, as small boys will. 'Piers used to torment me and physically bully me when we were small,' Jeremy later told the *Sunday Times*' 'Relative Values'. 'I remember him hitting me over the head repeatedly with a small, rubber yellow hammer. My mother couldn't leave us alone. Later on, he'd bully me psychologically – niggle, niggle, niggle – until I got into a rage and beat him to a pulp. He fought like a girl, so he was easy to overcome.'

Piers remembers something similar. 'My brother wasn't the most quick-witted of spanners,' he told the *Sunday Times*. 'He had a very short fuse; I found it amusing to light it and watch it explode. We were very competitive and my mother did everything to stop us fighting. I've just always loved verbal combat; my whole family are like that – rebellious, into debating and feuding. We're Irish Catholics. It gets fiery. I love it.'

Of course, the two are extremely close in age and it was clear, listening to both of them, that they were extremely pugnacious. Neither has ever been afraid of a tussle, albeit in very different fields: Piers in the world of celebrity and Jeremy out on the battlefield. But the existence of a younger brother was to give Piers a moral authority in later years, something he couldn't have dreamed about back then: when he was criticised for apparently not supporting the War on Iraq while he was editor of the *Mirror*. In his defence, he could point out that his own brother was serving in the Army and, naturally, he backed our boys; it was just the field in which they were fighting that he didn't like.

But the journalism bug bit very young, as did the bad habits that famously go along with it. 'I was really into newspapers at five or six, and used to point out the headlines that grabbed me,' Piers revealed in an interview with the *Independent*. 'I learned to read through the papers; whether this is good or bad, I have yet to work out. My parents ran the Griffin Inn and at Fletching C of E Primary, near Lewes, East Sussex, I was one of the few kids who every night went to the local pub. Ever since then, as a journalist, I have staggered to the pub after work.'

Indeed, he did more than that, helping his parents run their business from a very young age. 'I used to do the bottling up at 5am, then come to school,' he revealed in later years. 'I used to get in trouble for that [at school]. I think they thought I had an alcohol problem as a child.'

He maintains this is where his somewhat brash personality began to develop. Pubs are not places for quiet people and the young Piers was forced to fight to get heard. He succeeded, and began to develop a trademark style from an early age. 'I was always very cocky and noisy in the pub,' he admits. 'I loved holding forth, hearing the sound of my own voice, and a lot of people found it amusing so I just carried on.' It was a philosophy he was to continue into later life.

And he was a clever boy; although Piers would never shine academically, his achievements have been enough to defeat many a lesser man and required a good deal of native wit, something he possessed right from the start. 'Piers was unusually bright: at four he was reading Tolkien,' his brother Jeremy recalled. 'Later, he was into newspapers and Arsenal Football Club. I liked rugby, fishing and *Commando* magazine. We led independent lives, apart from cricket: we played it endlessly in our garden in Sussex. We became known at Sussex County Cricket ground – Imran Khan even invited us to the nets to bowl at him.'

Again, a reference to 'newspapers', something that was to surface repeatedly in stories about Piers' early life, and another early clue to his eventual destiny was that his birth father had also once been a journalist, although Piers did not discover this until he himself was an adult. It was on a visit to Ireland, where both sides of the family originated, that this came to light. 'There I was in the middle of southern Ireland in a place called Banagher and all these people came up to me, who had known my father,' Piers told *The Times*. 'His mother persuaded him to become a dentist because there was more money and security and all that, but it was interesting to find out that it's obviously in the blood, you know.' Indeed, it was there on both sides – his mother's father was a 'proper investigative journalist' on the *Sunday People* in the 1970s and it was this connection that would first introduce him to the world he was to dominate.

Piers always considered his stepfather Glynne to be his true father and emphasises that he treated him as if he were his own son. 'You know, he's been absolutely incredible,' he later said. 'He took on two young boys when he was in his twenties and did a great job for us. All four of us children had a lovely upbringing and a lot of fun. It wasn't privileged and we didn't have much money, but we had a great time.'

Another important family member was Piers' grandmother Margot, who looked after the children on a day-to-day basis while his parents ran the Griffin Inn. 'Unbelievably long hours, catering to maybe 200 people a day,' was how Piers described it. Within the family, Margot was known as 'Grande', and she and Piers have maintained an extremely close relationship; he has since dedicated one of his books to her and also moved his grandmother into one of his properties when she got older.

Gabrielle had a fair bit to contend with, not least because her son displayed an aptitude for the profession he was to make his own from early on. 'I was always incredibly nosy and fascinated by news,' he told the *Independent* in

2008. 'I also loved reading papers from a very early age. My mother remembers me pointing to a headline about a rape case when I was six and asking: "Mum, what does it mean when it says this girl was raped?" Quite a tricky enquiry to navigate for any parent.' But she managed, and Piers continued to be fascinated by news and how it was reported in the press.

Perhaps rather surprisingly to some, given the rough-and-tumble nature of the world he was to come to inhabit, first in journalism and then in show business, Piers was brought up a practising Catholic and attended church regularly. Further, he was given instruction in the religion by nuns, something he enjoyed.

'I don't want to overdo my devoutness because I think a proper devout Catholic would see me as pretty lapsed – it's just that my whole family, apart from my dad, are believers and that's the way we were brought up,' he told *The Times*. 'You'd just go along [to the nuns] and chat for an hour, and I liked the purity of the nuns and their pure view of life and the world. It was nice. I don't think that I've led such a pure life as those nuns, no. But I thought there was an idealistic side to them that was rather nice, you know. Always looking for the good in people is a nice trait to have.'

It was pretty much the polar opposite of what he himself would go on to do, but it hinted again at the more empathetic side of his character that was to make him an excellent interviewer once his television career proper took off.

Up to the age of seven, Piers attended Fletching Primary School in his home village, where he later recalled winning the 'Christmas decoration on your head' competition, before moving to Cumnor House and then Chailey, near Lewes in West Sussex. It was a bit of a comedown: Cumnor House was a private school, while Chailey was a comprehensive, but he coped with the change. 'I was very happy in my schools,' he recalled. 'I bounced between the two types of education; at seven, after the local primary, I went to a fee-paying prep school three miles away – Cumnor House – and was a boarder between eleven and thirteen. I noticed there was more money and it was better resourced. And there was daily sport – brilliant! A kid tossed a jar of magnesium into the swimming pool and blew it up. Although I'm now involved with the npower Climate Cops Campaign, in those days we weren't really aware of the environment, but I do remember thinking, that's not the most environment-friendly thing!'

In fact, his tone veered wildly when discussing his education; he found the transition from private to state school quite traumatic and had to endure some bullying, more of which below.

The young Piers was fairly typical in his television and radio tastes back then. Later, as an adult, he was asked what programmes he had enjoyed. '*Thunderbirds, Dallas, Dukes of Hazzard, Morecambe and Wise*, Selina Scott and all the big boxing fights,' he told the *Independent*. 'Try getting your shrink to analyse that little lot! As for radio,

I used to pretend to my schoolmates that I listened to John Peel, but of course listened instead to Peter Powell – who has transformed himself into one of the most successful talent agents in the country (well, he has to be, he manages me).'

It was standard fare for the 1960s and 70s, and revealed both mainstream tastes and a solid Middle England background. One of the secrets to Piers' success in all aspects of his life, from outrage over the Iraq War to his judging on ITV's *Britain's Got Talent*, is that he understands exactly what his audience/readership is thinking – because he is one of them.

Writing held an appeal from early on. When Piers was just fifteen, he wrote his first piece, a 1,500-word article about his village cricket team's visit to Malta for the *Mid Sussex Times*. For this, he was paid £15. 'I was so excited that I framed the cheque,' he later revealed on finding his forte. From then on, it was obvious what he planned to do.

And his education, after the local primary school, first at a private school and then a state one, was to stand him in good stead, as he admitted in a more positive reflection on his schooling. Both he and Jeremy completed their education that way round (whereas his two younger siblings attended state school first and were then educated privately) and he felt the experience had done him a power of good. 'I think my education was, in many ways, perfect,' he declared. 'I went to a great prep school until

I was thirteen and then I got my snobbish creases ironed out [at Chailey, near Lewes], where some of the kids did give me a hard time for being a posh twit.' His younger siblings suffered a lot of snobbery, he says, having come from the state sector.

This was, however, a more positive spin on events than he has portrayed at other times, as some bullying was taking place. The two boys in question had been taught to box in Canada. 'The first couple of punches when he smacked me in the face were really bad,' Piers told *The Times*, 'but after that I became completely immune to the pain and didn't feel anything else. And I think that's not bad as a template for life, really – the first couple of blows hurt, and then after that it's fine. And you just have to keep in there, fighting.'

In fact, the young Piers had more to deal with than he later liked to let on. In another interview, some years later, he admitted that it really hurt. Nor was it just a matter of a little kicking and punching. His new schoolmates labelled him 'Piss Puke Moron' (in later life, *Private Eye* magazine picked up on the 'Moron' tag, too), and he suddenly found himself in a very different educational world to the one he had just left. 'That was a big moment – and quite tough,' he explained. 'It upset my mum to have to do it, but we just ran out of money. Suddenly, to be yanked out of that gilded existence, with all your friends going to Eton and Westminster School, and you're going to the local comp, was a tricky time to navigate so I always understood the value of money and its precarious nature. Sometimes you have quite a lot of it, and the next moment, you haven't. Your life can be affected accordingly and moments like that do toughen you up.'

Indeed, given the fact that he was to run into trouble some years later on the back of what was seen as dubious share dealing (although there has never been any evidence of wrongdoing), it's easy to conclude this early brush with penury made him slightly reckless in some of his financial dealings, but he would still end up a rich man.

However much he might be able to laugh it off as an adult, the change of school was his second major childhood trauma. First, he had lost his father and now a change in his family's financial status meant that he lost out on the education for which he had seemed destined. Again, these early life experiences testify to a far more complex character than the one Piers likes to exude; he was forced to learn to cope, to bounce back and deal with altered circumstances. Nothing in his world could be taken for granted – perhaps other than the affection of his family – and, again, that brash exterior was as much a shield as anything else. He had to grow a thicker skin – and fast – if he was to survive this new, tougher environment and, as far back as that, he rose to the challenge and found he could cope.

His brother Jeremy also remembers going through a tough time. 'There were four of us children and my father could not educate us all privately, so Piers and I left our prep school for a comprehensive,' he said. 'Piers is a chameleon and he made friends with the largest boys there, who protected him. I found it harder to adjust. It was a good school, though, and we both did well.'

According to Piers, his brother was the one who protected him from even more of the toughness, albeit unwittingly. 'We both went to the local comp, where you'd get these skinheads who'd want to rearrange your face, so it was useful to say: "I'm not available for a fight, but my brother is,"' he told the *Sunday Times*. 'He got into scrapes and a lot of people used to wind him up. I'm not absolving myself from tormenting Jeremy, but he did have a volatile temper that manifested itself in extreme violence. The closer the British Army came to seizing his personage, the better for everyone.'

The boys were pretty self-sufficient, too, earning pocket money from a young age. 'We had a job share, filling bags with mushroom compost,' Jeremy recalls. 'We could make £6 per hour, split two ways. But Piers never liked getting his hands dirty, whereas I was always happy to get stuck in. I'm cautious, Piers thrives on risk. He managed to get us into the Members' Enclosure at the Oval when we were kids. We'd actually got into the commentators' box when Richie Benaud caught us and chased us out. We're different in our tastes in girls, too: Piers always liked skinny blondes and I've gone for more voluptuous brunettes.'

There were many other positive aspects to his life, too; all the early signs that Piers was being drawn to the written word continued to evolve during the course of his childhood and as he grew into his teens. In hindsight, it's easy to see it was inevitable that he should become a journalist, although at the time no one quite realised what greatness lay ahead.

'I remember getting a prize for handwriting; I had very good Italic handwriting,' Piers told the *Independent*. 'Now it's appalling, like a doctor's. I loved English and reading; I always liked non-fiction: biographies, stories of successful people. When I went to Chailey Comprehensive, they thought I was so far ahead in French that, at fourteen, I took the O-level and got a D. I retook it at fifteen and got a B, then retook it at sixteen to get an A. I then took the A-level and was awarded an O-level pass! So, I got four O-level passes in French. I got nine O-levels (more if you include my multiple French results).' Even so, it wasn't quite the same as his younger days. It wasn't just the fact that he had to get used to being called names and involved in rough housing; to put it bluntly, standards were not exactly what he was used to either.

'Chailey is one of the better comprehensives, but still had games only once a week,' he remembers. 'It had very good teachers: Miss Jones and Mr Shepherd together taught me the power of English language, literature and history. Mr Shepherd also taught Latin, but I was never much use.'

He would certainly go on to flex the power of the English language, not just as a newspaper editor but as a television presenter, too. That, however, was still some decades off.

The next educational establishment that Piers attended was Lewes Priory sixth-form college, where he began to prove that he was perhaps not all that academically inclined. 'When I went on to Lewes Priory sixth-form college, they made you take another O-level while you were doing your A-levels,' he remembers. 'I did Italian, hoping that my Latin would help, but they said they had never had a student who, after taking Latin, had done so badly in Italian: I got a U – ungraded!' This information was paraded with typical panache, though: when Piers failed at something, and he was to encounter a good many setbacks in later life, he made a joke out of it. He was a natural fighter and had been from a young age.

Piers had happy memories of his later school years, however – or at least he said he did. 'I was probably most fond of Mr Freeman, who taught history A-level,' he revealed. 'He was cruel, but fair. "Your boy is a buffoon," was his entire report to my parents one year. He probably thinks subsequent events have borne him out. It was a great school, a hotbed of rock music and gambling. I ran three-card brag games in the common room and we played bridge (weird for seventeen-year-olds). I got an A in English, a B in history and a C in French [retake]. It was wine, women and song (all my schools were co-ed), a perfect background for a journalism course.'

Even so, the course was not exactly his first choice. That C grade in French was a retake; had he passed the exam first time around, he would have gone to Warwick

University, but then the world might never have heard of Susan Boyle.

Immediately after leaving school, the young Piers spent a short time with Lloyd's of London, the insurance specialists. This was, after all, the early 1980s: the time of the yuppie, the brick-sized mobile phone and the Stock Exchange's 'Big Bang', when an awful lot of young men and women worked in finance before moving on to what they really wanted to do. Piers later said he found it 'boring', but this seemed, briefly, to be the life for which his background had prepared him: a double-barrelled surname, an early stint at public school and the desire to make money. He was also an admirer of Margaret Thatcher and voted for her as soon as he became eligible to do so: 'I thought she was a great leader for most of her reign, but then, like most of them, she went slightly potty,' he later declared.

But that stint at Lloyd's was to last less than two years. A great many yuppies were to discover that their real interest lay elsewhere and, with Piers, it didn't take too long. Besides, journalism already had him within its grasp. Courtesy of his grandfather, there was some family background in the profession and Piers had also experienced the thrill of having his first piece published and seeing his words in print. Now it was just a question of learning how to do things properly, and so he was off to journalism school.

'The Journalism Centre at Harlow College had a very good NCTJ one-year course, with 1,000 applicants for

50-plus places,' he remembers. 'There were 51 girls and two of the five blokes lived in London so weren't around much: 17:1! My shorthand was up to 100 words a minute; I'd be a very good secretary. Studying the law of libel and slander was very useful. Everyone on that course got a job on a local newspaper. I was the last because I insisted on London – I'd been told the stories were juiciest in London and could be sold to the national papers. I had been going to Warwick University but liked the lure of the bright lights of journalism. I'd like my kids to go to university.'

And he had to pay his own way; Piers' family might have been slightly upper-crust but they were not rich (he'd already had to change schools) and they could not afford to fund his education further without him contributing something. In the summer he would work logging trees for £35 a day. 'I developed very large forearms and nearly died when a giant conifer fell the wrong way and missed my head by three inches,' he later revealed.

Relations with his brother improved massively (as well as foreshadowing another famous Piers Morgan stance). 'Once I left home at 18 to join the Army, we became closer,' Jeremy told the *Sunday Times*. 'Piers left home before me, to work at Lloyd's in London, then to do journalism at Harlow College. I'd been stationed in Northern Ireland, the Balkans and Bosnia before I went to Basra in 2004; Piers was editing the *Mirror* then. He was adamant we shouldn't go to war; I was adamant we should, to rid the world of Saddam and WMD [Weapons of Mass Destruction]. I used to call Piers a "cheese-eating surrender monkey".'

Many journalists begin by plying their trade on local newspapers and that is exactly what happened next. Piers left Harlow to work at the Surrey and South London Newspaper Group, where he was a reporter on the *South London Press*. Humble as it sounds, this kind of background – learning how to dig up stories and make such mundane events such as the village fête sound interesting – can prove an invaluable training. Not that he had much to do with local events; it might have been a provincial newspaper, but it was in the nation's capital city and so, from early on, Piers reported on major news. He was finding out about real life stories, too.

This was the time of the Brixton riots, which Piers covered for the *Streatham and Tooting News*. It was also his job to interview a prostitute. 'Your life must be terrible,' he told her.

What are you talking about?' came the indignant reply. 'How often do you get your leg over every week? I love it, and I love the nice fur coat and the nice flat. How dare you patronise me like that!'

It was a spirited reaction, and also proved that Piers had a gift for getting people to make revealing, sometimes outrageous comments. The experience proved invaluable; it was 'a brilliant insight', he said into not pre-judging any given situation and also taught him how to get a story.

'The number-one thing I look for in any journalist is

charm,' he said in later years. 'It's not best results, it's not a university degree, it's not anything. If they can come into my office and charm me, they can charm anyone.'

He was on his way.

CHAPTER TWO

BIZARRE

Piers Morgan was a young man with a lot of energy that would soon stand him in good stead. Already he was doing well, learning his trade on the local *South London Press*, but he also showed a knack for making the most of his situation that would pitch him into a role on one of the most successful newspapers of the day.

'He was a natural,' explained Joan Mulcaster, then associate editor of the *Sutton Herald*. 'He was very, very bright, and right from the start he grasped what the job required. He had this knack of being able to get old ladies to talk to him. Once he was sent on a story, he was sure to succeed.' The only problem, according to Mulcaster, was that Piers didn't get on with the then editor, 'because he was too good, and he knew it.' He was clearly destined for greater things.

There was the hard news angle for a start, which began with the Brixton riots. 'I saw the pressure building in communities,' Piers told *The Times* in 1999. 'There's a similar situation now. I think there'll be real payback. In the cities you have got total lawlessness on the streets. It's not necessarily there in the figures, but in terms of an underclass of kids abandoned by the establishment and by their fathers in some cases. The gangs are all they have. Thirty kids stabbed on the streets of London last year doesn't tell me crime is getting any better.'

As well as interviewing colourful locals, he was sharp enough to see that celebrities who did pantomime at Wimbledon's theatre – among them Cliff Richard, Rowan Atkinson and Frank Bruno – were of interest to a far wider audience than those served by the paper he was working on. It wasn't long before he secured little chats with them, wrote them up into a story and then sold them on to the national press.

He started doing the odd shift for the national papers, too, after Joan Mulcaster introduced him to a former *Sutton Herald* reporter, Kevin O'Sullivan, who was now working for the *Sun*. 'You don't want to touch the shit I'm writing,' O'Sullivan told him, but Piers, who was made of sterner stuff, responded, 'I'm not too proud.' And so it was that he found himself doing the odd shift on Britain's biggest-selling daily (and dropping the 'Pughe' part of his surname – he said it made his by-line too long, but in fact it was completely out of character with working for the *Sun*).

And it wasn't long before he came to the attention of Kelvin MacKenzie, then editor of the *Sun*. At the time,

MacKenzie was one of the best-known and most influential editors; his *Sun* was responsible for such headlines as STICK IT UP YOUR JUNTA, FREDDIE STARR ATE MY HAMSTER and UP YOURS, DELORS. MacKenzie, too, had a brash personality which made itself felt in the newspaper he ran. In short, there could be no better place for a fiercely ambitious journalist with the popular touch to begin making his name.

MacKenzie quickly hired Piers, and after a year he became editor of the 'Bizarre' column and displayed a gift for self-promotion that took even fellow journalists by surprise. It was a time of massive change: the late eighties was seeing considerably less interest in the established fodder of the gossip columns, the aristocracy (with the enormous exception of Diana, Princess of Wales), and far more excitement about celebrities. 'Bizarre', launched several years earlier by another extremely colourful and brilliant journalist, John Blake, was a gossip column focusing on celebrities and was to kick-start a spectacular career.

What Piers did was breathtakingly simple: he put himself in the photo with the stars. Instead of just photographing a pop star talking about his latest single, he would run a picture of himself talking to the star about his latest single. This manoeuvre had two outcomes: it put Piers on the same level as the pop star, making him out to be another member of the star's celebrity world, while at the same time causing him to become massively recognisable to readers.

Few journalists ever become visible to the wider world outside their immediate profession and become famous in their own right, but Kelvin MacKenzie had achieved this and now his young protégé was having a go at it, too.

According to Piers, it was all Kelvin's idea, and started with a picture of him with Bros, the pop-star duo who were famous at the time. 'I was amazed when Kelvin used the picture giant-sized on the centre spread,' he said. 'That was when he said to me, "Right, get alongside all the stars. I don't care how you do it, just do it." All I did was carry it out.

'I became the Friend of the Stars, a rampant egomaniac, pictured all the time with famous people – Madonna, Stallone, Bowie, Paul McCartney – hundreds of them,' he continued. 'It was shameless as they didn't know me from Adam. The *Sun* had had a bad time after losing an action with Elton John, but this was harmless and funny. The publicity people from the record companies were all in on the joke. I got a letter one day from someone on HMS *Campbeltown*, saying I was appalling. Everyone on board got in a rage when they saw my face – so I printed that letter in full, in the column. I had four great years, travelling the world.'

And the stars themselves were usually only too happy to play along. They knew the deal: they were getting as much publicity as anyone, which could only benefit their careers and it certainly wasn't doing anyone any harm. On one occasion, Piers was shown presenting a platinum disc to

Gloria Estefan: 'We should be giving you this, Piers, after all the support you have given us over the last two years,' said Gloria's husband, Emilio.

'Thanks for everything,' added Gloria. 'You and the *Sun* have been wonderful to us.'

'As I pointed out to rock's most charming couple,' wrote Piers, 'that's what friends are for.'

And it was all down to MacKenzie. The two men formed an instant bond. Piers went on to describe him (accurately) as a 'dangerous genius', while Kelvin encouraged his twenty-three-year-old hot shot to come up with outrageous stories and to push himself in the frame alongside whoever he was interviewing. 'The headline instantly became "Piers Morgan 687pt, Bizarre 4pt",' Kelvin said in later years, referring to the size of Piers' by-line compared to that of the column itself, but his editor was happy with what he was doing, as was Piers himself. It was also at this stage that Piers first made the acquaintance of Max Clifford, one of the best-known publicists of the age and with whom he was to have many dealings in the years ahead.

It was this trio – Piers, Kelvin and Max – who came up with one bombshell after another. 'What was different about that period was that the *Sun* under Kelvin MacKenzie suddenly decided to take celebrities like pop stars, footballers and all the rest of them, pull them from the back pages and the gossip columns on to the front page as news stories,' Piers later told the *Guardian*. 'Max was the easiest guy to deal with. He'd say, "Look, mate, a nod's as good as a wink. He only hit him once, but if you want it three times, that's fine." Nowadays the PCC [Press Complaints Commission] would frown on that. From Max's point of view, it makes it slightly trickier.'

Not that it really had to be a bombshell; by now, the public was completely obsessed by celebrity, so much so that practically anything to do with anyone on TV would sell. 'A typical Max "Bizarre" story used to involve an *EastEnders*' star having a meal at the Red Fort curry house, then having a fight at Xenon nightclub – all of which he represented,' recalled Piers. 'It was much more lawless then. The idea that someone like Max could create the entire story around his people, it wouldn't be as easy now.'

It was also at this stage of his career that Piers first became involved with the Press Complaints Commission (PCC) because inevitably his attitude towards his job could be summed up as 'absolutely anything goes' but it was all invaluable experience. By now, he was building up contacts, learning his trade and earning a name for himself into the bargain – and all while still in his twenties.

This period also shaped Piers' attitude towards the editorship of a newspaper. Kelvin MacKenzie, one of the most fearless editors of his generation, took no prisoners and his style would clearly influence his protégé in the future. Given the nature of their professions, both men were adamant that they themselves were fair game and were prepared to push the boat out in a way other editors refused to do. What's more, both paid the price one way or another – MacKenzie eventually had to leave the *Sun*, while Piers was very publicly sacked from the *Mirror* – but both raised their heads above the parapet in a way few other editors would have dared.

'I think that, if you are a tabloid editor, then you deserve everything you get, frankly. I have no right to privacy,' Kelvin told the *Independent* many years later, as he looked back over his career. 'You have got to understand where you lie in the ladder of life. I have absolutely no doubts about where I am. It would be somewhere near the bottom. It may be at the bottom. I always thought when editing the *Sun* that the greatest journalistic act I could perform would be actually exposing myself so you'd end up with a headline: SUN EDITOR IN THREE-IN-A BED SCANDAL. And you'd start with an intro: 'Kelvin MacKenzie wept with shame last night as it was revealed...' I think the idea that editors are in some way part of the Establishment is just plain wrong. I sort of drifted in and out of that. The idea that the Prime Minister would ask you what you thought about something is truly, truly absurd.'

In fact, a number of prime ministers were to ask both MacKenzie and his young protégé for their advice because the other attribute they shared was the common touch (in other words, what the man on the Clapham omnibus might think). Each had a good sense of what their readers wanted (although in both cases there were errors: on Kelvin's part, most notoriously in the case of the *Sun*'s coverage of the Hillsborough disaster, and then there were the faked Iraqi War pictures in Piers' case). Neither was in any way remotely deferential to any sort of authority and both were only too happy to challenge the existing status quo. Their political views were broadly similar, too, despite the fact that Piers would go on to edit the *Sun*'s rival and its opposite number on the political spectrum: Kelvin was extremely right wing, while Piers was mildly right wing. Both made waves, both got what they wanted and, even outside the narrow world in which they lived, both were often talked about. And Piers was well aware who he had to thank for his success: 'I owe it all to Kelvin,' he stated, when he eventually left the *Sun*. 'He's always been there for me.'

In the midst of making a name for himself professionally, Piers also married for the first time in July 1991, in Hampshire. The lady in question was a nurse – Marion Shalloe – and she was to bear him three sons. Being in his mid-twenties, he was perhaps a little young to settle down and, indeed, the marriage would not last but at this stage it seemed as if he was determined to do everything faster, younger and better than anyone else. He was a married man, already becoming a famous journalist and, two years later, the couple's first son, Spencer William, was born in 1993.

But Piers' lifestyle was not conducive to settling down. To write his column – and, indeed, for the best part of the two decades that he would spend on Fleet Street – he had to put in unfeasibly long hours, on top of which, as a celebrity gossip columnist, he had to make regular appearances at numerous show-business events. Marion is one of the few subjects that Piers is a little reticent about, although he has talked in the past about being a less than perfect husband and also owned up to feelings of guilt. He was, after all, brought up as a practising Catholic and divorce goes against his beliefs.

But back at 'Bizarre', he was going from strength to strength and proving that he could quite effortlessly attract publicity: for example, as far back as 1989, Ben Elton publicly criticised him for implying they were friends. (In fact, Piers pretty much implied that he was friends with *everyone* in those days.)

Almost everyone, that is; a couple of years later, Donnie Wahlberg of the pop group New Kids On The Block wore a T-shirt emblazoned with the legend 'Piers Morgan Sucks' on stage. 'In case you didn't know this dude Piers Morgan, he writes for a newspaper called the *Sun*,' Donnie informed his audience. 'He's always slagging us off and putting us down – his stuff should be ignored. You shouldn't read what he writes in that newspaper.'

Piers, ever ready to indulge in a feud even then, rose to the challenge. 'Donnie's sense of humour is obviously as atrocious as his singing,' he said smoothly. 'I can't understand it. I thought we were great friends. Perhaps this has something to do with our recent reports that the New Kids and Mr Wahlberg in particular were washed up.

I hope he doesn't intend being a comedian when, or if, he grows up.'

But it was not the end of that particular saga. In an excellent demonstration of the way in which Piers managed over and over to make himself the centre of the story, nine months later he was pictured with Donnie again. This time, the latter was full of remorse and contrition. 'I've done some stupid things in the last two years, but now I've grown up,' said Donnie. 'I did it on the spur of the moment, because all the British fans seemed to hate you. Now I realise they all read your column, every damned one of them. It's the same with me. A lot of people say they hate me, but they all buy my records.'

As a *mea culpa*, this was some going, but Donnie clearly realised that he was at a stage in his career when he could do with some support from the press. Two decades on, with Piers about to become one of the most powerful men on American television (where Donnie still appears), he was clearly right.

Piers was clearly in his element; there were now reports of Irish singing star Sinéad O'Connor ringing up to talk to him about her marriage breakdown. In 1992, there was one bizarre (appropriately enough) incident involving Madonna. Piers devoted most of a page to the 'world's best singer and columnist', who had turned up in a limo for a chat at his office in Wapping. A couple of days later came an apology from Piers for having been duped by a lookalike and a few days after that came the claim that he himself had hired the lookalike and the apology was a joke.

When Piers was required to play dirty, he would do so. In 1993, the singer Holly Johnson of Frankie Goes To Hollywood revealed that he was HIV positive, something much feared and little understood back then. Piers was one of the first with the story but he hadn't got it himself. Rather, Holly gave an interview to *The Times Magazine* – but *The Times*, like the *Sun*, was owned by Rupert Murdoch and based in the same premises in Wapping, East London. Piers might have been coy about how he'd stumbled on his exclusive but it wasn't so hard to guess.

He was also extremely good at being in the right place at the right time. May 1993 saw him in Monte Carlo at the World Music Awards, where he had a ringside view of a spat between supermodels Carla Bruni (now married to President Nicolas Sarkozy) and Claudia Schiffer over Prince Albert of Monaco. According to Piers, Carla won. Headed up by a headline that read: I SAW SCHEMING CARLA NICK CLAUDIA'S PRINCE, the piece also had a large strapline, which read: 'Piers Morgan is at the next table as the catfight fur flies'.

Again, he managed to place himself at the centre of the story: 'Supermodels Claudia Schiffer and Carla Bruni fought like cat and cat over Prince Albert of Monaco at the World Music Awards in Monte Carlo,' he rather breathlessly began. A piece then followed about the two women shooting daggers at one another. Claudia, who had been dating Prince Albert, was initially sitting beside him throughout the awards (and near Michael Jackson), but, when forced to leave her seat to present an award, Carla lost no time in bagging said seat for herself. Claudia claimed it back, only to lose out once again at the subsequent dinner at the Hotel de Paris, when Carla managed to end up beside the Prince, who, according to Piers, 'looked like the cat who took his pick of two bowls of cream'.

Michael Jackson was also present that evening, with a companion who didn't attract too much notice at the time, but that was in May 1993. By the August, a criminal investigation had begun into allegations that Jackson had sexually abused a teenage boy called Jordan Chandler. Piers suddenly realised he'd been eyewitness to another big story. Unearthing the photos of the night in question, there was Michael with a young boy on his knee – a relationship that had been widely known about, although until then the implication had been that Michael was actually acting as the child's surrogate father (and, indeed, the accusations have never been proven, not least because Jackson unwisely decided to pay the family off in possibly the worst decision of his career).

True to form, Piers not only published the inside details of the event in question, in which he referred to the child as 'Jordan Schwartz' (Schwartz was, in fact, the name of his stepfather), but again placed himself at the centre of it all. 'I watched stars' horror as Jacko cuddled the boy,' he proclaimed, with an accompanying photograph of Michael Jackson with Jordan on his knee. Of course, this was to be an even bigger story as it marked the start of the slow decline of one of the world's most famous entertainers.

Piers' natural instinct for a story was otherwise serving him well. 'Jordan giggled as the superstar singer hugged and cuddled him in front of a huge VIP audience and millions of TV viewers,' he solemnly proclaimed. 'Their extraordinary antics were the talk of the celebrity-packed room at Monte Carlo's famous Sporting Club.' There followed dark remarks from various unnamed celebrities – 'It was disgusting. I wouldn't let him anywhere near a son of mine' – while Piers himself commented on how uncomfortable it looked and how he wouldn't have been at all happy had Jordan been his own child.

No one quite knew how big this particular story was to grow, but Piers was now proving that his news sense was sharper than it had ever been. Nor was it just Kelvin MacKenzie who was delighted that his young hiring had turned out to be such a success; the ultimate owner of the *Sun*, Rupert Murdoch, was also beginning to notice his antics. Here was a reporter with not just promise and flair but also an ability to be in the right place at the right time. He was beginning to stand head and shoulders above the rest.

But it wasn't all solemn allegations. The next partner in the celebrity dance that Piers was creating around himself was Chris Evans. At that stage, Evans was building up his own career the first time round, making a name for himself on Channel 4's *The Big Breakfast*. He had refused an interview unless Piers beat him at tennis; Piers duly obliged and soon Chris was confiding in him. I'VE COURT YOU, EVANS, blasted the headline, followed by, 'Chris has to spill the beans after I smash him at tennis.' Evans himself was very similar to Piers: both were brash young men, eager to make names for themselves in the media, and, like Piers, Evans was to blow the opportunity only to get a second chance.

'There were various embarrassing questions I wanted to ask *Big Breakfast* star Chris during our interview – questions he said he had no intention of answering unless I beat him at tennis,' began Piers. 'So the scene was set.' The duo adjourned to the Harbour Club in West London and, minutes later, Chris was telling Piers, 'Bob's great. I've only seen him about four or five times, but he's a good laugh.' The 'Bob' in question was Bob Geldof, whose company – Planet 24 – owned *The Big Breakfast*.

There were, however, a good many examples in the course of the chat that showed both the volatility of Evans' nature – something that would seriously derail his career and from which he has only recently recovered – and Piers' own ability to extract highly revealing anecdotes from his subjects. Back then, Chris Evans was still something of an unknown quantity but stories were beginning to circulate, including one to the effect that he had been sacked from Radio Piccadilly in Manchester for making jokes about eating a cat. 'He [the controller] said it was offensive to cat-owners and that I was a little shit, who would be fired if I said anything like that again,' revealed Chris. 'So I walked out on the spot instead.' It was far from being the last time that Evans walked out on a job, a habit that was in danger of damaging his career.

He was also forthcoming about his days as a kissogram. 'It was purely business,' he said. 'Other kissogram agencies at that time were charging £18 a time and there wasn't one in my hometown of Warrington so I started up at £6 a time and we promptly built up a massive clientele.'

If that were not enough, both Piers and Chris proved themselves to have the common touch: a knack for the kind of story that would not only amuse but also make the reader think they were talking to one of their own. Asked what his most embarrassing act as a star had been, Evans replied, 'It was a charity thing I did for Roy Castle last year. There were 26,000 people there, and they wanted me to dress up as a schoolboy and aim a catapult at this stunning model's bottom. I remember saying to the organisers, "I'll do it because it's for charity, but I hope you realise I wouldn't if you were paying me any amount of money..."' Game, set and match to both of them.

Piers was by then becoming such a celebrity in his own right that he was accorded the ultimate accolade of being the victim of the 'gunge tank' on BBC1's *Noel's House Party*, when viewers had to choose between him and the *Daily Mirror*'s Rick Sky (his predecessor on 'Bizarre')

– they eventually plumped for Piers. 'The nation's lost its taste,' he sighed, while being 'gunged'.

This was later picked up by the *Independent*, who referred to his 'hideously self-reverential' column in the *Sun*. So it might have been, but the technique was also bringing the writer his own level of fame. By this point, the satirical magazine *Private Eye* had certainly noticed him, currently dubbing him Piers 'Gormless' Morgan, a nickname that might have been amusing but, it must be said, was far from true.

Events were showing Piers to be a really talented journalist, one who within the space of a few short years had gone from being a complete beginner to a person more than capable of holding his own among the celebrities he interviewed. He might not yet have become a household name (indeed, this was some years away), but *Sun* readers knew him, as did the celebrities with whom he mingled and so, most importantly, did Rupert Murdoch, one of the world's most powerful media barons.

Piers' timing, as ever, could not have been better for what was to happen next. He had learned his trade at the hands of a master, Kelvin MacKenzie. Now he was as adept as any at practising some of the darker arts associated with his profession, and he was capable of not only nosing out a story but also of creating one himself pretty much out of thin air, often with himself in the centre of it. He was a seriously talented journalist and great things were expected of him.

At the same time, over at the *News Of The World* – a Sunday tabloid with the country's biggest circulation, also owned by one R. Murdoch – crises had been rumbling on the backburner. In December 1993, the paper's editor Patsy Chapman (in situ since 1988) signed off ill. The paper's deputy – Stuart Higgins – had been standing in for her, but now a merry-go-round of job shifts was about to take place. And so, in January 1994, Kelvin MacKenzie stepped down from his colossally successful tenure at the *Sun* and became managing editor of BSkyB television, which was also Murdoch-owned but would not suit him anywhere near as well as the *Sun*. Higgins stepped across to become editor of the *Sun*, while, at the *News Of The World*, it was now obvious that Chapman would not be coming back.

This left a vacancy and so, to the sound of jaws dropping all over Fleet Street, Murdoch promoted twenty-eight-year-old Piers Morgan to the editor's chair, making him the youngest editor of a national newspaper in over fifty years. Technically, he was 'acting editor' (the situation with Patsy Chapman was treated with some sensitivity), but in reality he had managed to nab the top job.

Piers himself was away at the time and was as staggered – and delighted – as anyone else. Usually, it took decades on Fleet Street to reach the very top and yet there he was, after a mere five years, editing the country's biggest name.

'I don't think anything will beat walking on Miami Beach in 1994, age twenty-eight, barefoot in the surf, and getting a call from Rupert Murdoch as he politely informed me I was going to be running the biggest newspaper in the world,' he admitted afterwards, and, for all the subsequent glories, you would be hard put not to suspect this is a view he holds to this day. At the time, however, he kept things dignified. 'I am delighted to be given this tremendous opportunity,' he said. 'The *News Of The World* is a national institution and I am eagerly looking forward to the exciting challenge of acting as its editor.'

But this was not the first time that he had been offered a new job. In 1993, Kelvin MacKenzie had offered him the post of assistant editorship of the *Sun*, but Piers had turned it down. 'I just didn't want to do it then,' he said later. 'I wasn't ready and I thought I contributed more by staying on "Bizarre".' But this was different; 'Bizarre' itself was also turning into a sort of kingmaker for editors: founder John Blake had gone on to become editor of the *People*, while another 'Bizarre editor' (Martin Dunn) ended up in the top chair of *Today* and, subsequently, the *New York Daily News*.

As Piers would later put it, in some ways, 'Bizarre' was a newspaper-within-a-newspaper and so good training for the next step. 'Obviously, Kelvin had helped, but you have to realise I was filling the column five days a week, running it like a mini-newspaper,' he recalled. 'I had a staff of four and my own budget. I had been offered promotion as features editor of the *Sun*, but turned it down, feeling I wasn't ready yet to be a faceless executive.'

A telling remark, for Piers was never ready to be a faceless anything.

The appointment might have caused widespread astonishment, but those who really knew Piers were convinced he was up to the job. 'Piers is arrogant and ambitious,' said Rick Sky, his predecessor on 'Bizarre' and now a rival columnist at the *Daily Mirror*. 'But in our world, that's no criticism. He's a good operator and he shouldn't be underestimated. He will surprise everyone.'

Piers himself was (uncharacteristically) modest but he knew just the opportunity that now lay ahead. 'I'll just do my best,' he declared, as the news became public. 'You don't have to be an expert. When I went to "Bizarre", I said I knew nothing about pop music. All these years on, I still don't know anything about pop music but I know how to make the column work for readers.'

And he would go on to prove that he knew exactly how to make the *News Of The World* work for its readers, too.

Piers was called upon to hit the ground running, and so he did; he might have felt nervous behind the scenes but he wasn't about to show it. 'When you're the editor of a paper, you've got to exude absolute confidence from the moment you get in to the moment you go to bed because, if you don't, the staff are going to be, "Oh God, he doesn't know what he's doing!" I had to pretend I knew what I was doing, even if I didn't,' he revealed later on.

In the meantime, he had to get his team together – and fast. Journalist Sue Carroll had been deputy editor of the *News Of The World* and had also been stepping into Patsy Chapman's shoes, as and when necessary. Now she was offered an executive post but turned it down and left the paper. Rather ironically, several years later and after a stint at the *Sun*, she was to end up as the *Mirror*'s star columnist, but Piers himself had made an effort to get her to stay, something that smoothed the way for their relationship further down the line.

Instead, Phil Hall was taken on as Piers' deputy. With a background on the *People* and the *Sunday Express*, he was felt to have a strong news background. Meanwhile, the cavalcade thundered on: in June, it was announced that Patsy was not coming back, and Piers was promoted from acting editor to the real thing, although, in fact, everyone had known, right from the start, that he was the de facto guy in charge.

Circulation, the lifeblood of any newspaper, began to rise and, with it, Piers Morgan's star. His tenure at the *News Of The World* was to prove a controversial one but, as so often in his career, he managed to be right in the middle of the action – just as it was all going on.

CHAPTER THREE

ALL THE NEWS THAT'S FIT TO PRINT

Piers Morgan was now in the chair of the *News Of The World*, Britain's biggest-selling daily. Right from the start, he had jumped in with both feet and showed he had what it takes. And he clearly wasn't willing to tolerate the old Fleet Street ways, in which lunch lasted the best part of the day; on his arrival, long-serving staff were somewhat dismayed to read a notice telling them to confine lunch to one hour from then on. 'A few had been in the habit of having the traditional Fleet Street liquid lunch,' observed Piers, rather primly for him. 'I've only been a journalist seven years, so all I know is the new-style journalism.' But his always excellent timing really couldn't be bettered at this juncture for, right in front of him, one of the biggest stories of the decade was unfolding.

Indeed, it was a story that was to cover more than one decade, for it concerned the Prince and Princess of Wales. The pair had married in 1981, amid much talk about the 'stuff of which fairytales are made', and promptly went about disproving anything of the sort. After producing Princes William (1982) and Harry (1984), the royal marriage had fallen apart and, in December 1992, it was announced that the couple were to separate. Princess Diana drove newspaper sales as no one had ever done before and, in the wake of the royal separation, fascination in her only grew, much to the advantage of the press, who charted every twist and turn in her life story. Of course, at that time, no one knew the story was to end in tragedy but there was a huge appetite, among both journalists and readers, for anything at all to do with Diana.

It was in August 1994 that Piers' *News Of The World* broke a story that not only dominated the news agenda but also began to hint for the first time at quite the extent of Diana's collaboration with the press. When Andrew Morton's book *Diana: Her True Story* was published in June 1992, it had caused uproar but it was not until Diana's death that it was revealed she had been closely involved with it all. Now, for the first time ever, she was caught out briefing a journalist – and all because of Piers.

The story that precipitated the huge row ran in the *News Of The World*. It alleged that art dealer Oliver Hoare had been subject to 300 nuisance phone calls, some picked up by his wife, who then involved the police. The police discovered the calls originated from Kensington Palace and, more specifically, Diana herself, at which point a senior unnamed politician stepped in to persuade them to drop the case to avoid further embarrassment.

It was no sooner published than several interested parties swung into motion. First, inevitably, there were concerns that it was Prince Charles' camp deliberately planting stories to make his wife look bad, a view that would appear to have been supported by Diana herself. A huge story appeared in the next day's *Daily Mail* – under the headline WHAT HAVE I DONE TO DESERVE THIS? – in which friends of the Princess claimed there were people out there who were trying to make her appear unstable. 'I feel I am being destroyed,' she told journalist Richard Kay. 'There is absolutely no truth in it.'

However, on the same day, the *Sun* (the *News Of The World*'s stable-mate) carried the headline QUEEN'S FURY AT PLOTTING DIANA, with a picture showing the Princess getting into a car with Richard Kay. His by-line had been on many stories involving Diana, always with a sympathetic angle and almost invariably quoting 'Friends of the Princess'. Finally, this picture proved what many had long suspected, namely the so-called 'friends' were none other than the Princess herself. In this particular instance, she had been briefing Kay about the angle to take to rebut the claims, on top of which Kay himself had rung Piers on the Saturday before the story was due to break to make the Princess's case. Diana subsequently went on to claim that she had made her own investigations and discovered a little boy (unnamed) who lived in Kensington Palace was the real culprit, but it was pretty obvious to everyone else what had really gone on.

Scarcely a day went by without a new 'Diana' story at this point, but this particular piece really stood out, as it involved a politician stepping in. It was hinted to be either Nicholas Soames (unlikely, since he is a close friend of Prince Charles) or William Waldegrave (who had links to the royals), but the identity of the man in question was never made clear. Then there was the minor matter of how such an extremely detailed story made its way into the public domain with widespread suspicion that it had been leaked by the police, although Piers would not be drawn. 'Suffice it to say, this is a story which has been fairly common knowledge in the police for some time,' was all he would admit. The affair itself had also been widely suspected by Fleet Street, but this was the first time there was some real proof.

It crowned Piers as the king of scandal – life and blood to a newspaper like the *News Of The World* – and was the culmination of a stunning successful six months in the editor's chair. This was the biggest story he'd run to date, but it was by no means the only one: since taking on the editor's mantle, he'd revealed Tory MP Hartley Booth's relationship with former researcher Emily Barr, leading to Booth's resignation from a junior government post. He then published a similar piece about Labour MP Dennis Skinner (THE BEAST OF LEGOVER), and also revealed the affair between Lady Bienvenida Buck, then married to another Tory MP, Anthony Buck, and the Chief of the Defence Staff Sir Peter Harding – who was also forced to resign – but topped that with a story about the Tory MP Alan Clark's affairs with a mother, Valerie Harkess, and her two daughters, Josephine and Alison, whom he'd nicknamed 'The Coven'. The injured husband and father, James, posed with a horsewhip and admitted he would like to use it on the great man himself.

This was an impressive tally by any standards but it was the royal stories where Piers really came into his own: his first 'Diana' story was that her psychiatric records had been stolen; this was followed up by the Hoare piece, which in turn led to a story from one James Hewitt, to the effect that he'd been the recipient of silent phone calls, too. Then came material about Diana's affair with Hewitt, still not widely known about at the time.

All of this mattered, not just for the entertainment of the nation but because Piers was still so very young. There had been plenty of grumbling about a lack of experience when he'd first got the job and yet, from the moment he took up the post, he'd been all but setting the news agenda. Meanwhile, he was careful to praise his reporters. 'They are the ones who bring in the stories,' he told *The Spectator*. 'This isn't false modesty; the only credit I would take is having the balls to run the stories.'

Royal stories, especially those involving Diana, could be tricky to handle, too. Despite the public's voracious appetite for anything involving 'Shy Di' (who came close to bringing the Monarchy down), they adored her and, while they would read scandalous stories about her, there was a line over which no paper nor editor should step. Alleging nuisance calls while maintaining a sympathetic aura wasn't that easy, and there was a big risk in becoming the first paper to reveal Diana's own extra-marital affairs but the *News Of The World* somehow managed to pull it off.

'On the Hewitt-Diana story, I held a council of war with my three top executives,' recalled Piers. 'I often do this because I'm only twenty-nine years old and I'm aware I have experienced journalists around, but I do have to make the final decision.'

Then there was the issue of the Monarchy itself. At the time, the Republican movement in Britain was not a strong one but sometimes newspapers running anti-Windsor stories, especially those owned by the Australian-born Republican Rupert Murdoch, were accused of base motives. Piers, however, was having none of it.

'I totally believe in the Monarchy as an institution,' he declared, 'but I don't agree with royals behaving like the rest of us. If we're going to give them palaces to live in, then they should behave in a regal manner. Princess Diana's come out of it well... she's loved more than she ever was.

'My ultimate defence of stories is that they are 100 per cent true. I don't make moral judgements. Sometimes my mother rings up and tells me to leave Diana alone. My grandmother will say, "That's a revolting load of rubbish you printed this morning," but, when I press her further, she will admit she found it entertaining.'

And so did everyone else.

Piers didn't usually bring his age into anything and he sounded far more himself when defending the publication of the Bienvenida Buck/Sir Peter Harding story, described by some people as a 'sad' case. Sir Peter had been forced to resign from his post and his estranged wife had been pictured looking distraught.

'I don't think he's a sad case at all!' insisted Piers. 'I'd do the same thing again tomorrow. He was the Chief of the Defence Staff, behaving in a way that was quite appallingly stupid for a man in his position and also compromising the job he was doing. All army officers had only recently been sent a memo saying that adultery would result in dismissal, yet, while the Gulf War was raging, he was wining and dining his mistress. It was hypocritical. I'm no great moraliser but I think it's wrong for people in positions of power to commit adultery if, by so doing, they leave themselves or their jobs exposed. And it's wrong if they're preaching one thing and doing another.

'I'm not dictating to ordinary people but say a married woman sleeps with the village policeman, her husband finds out, there's a fight and someone tells the *News Of The World* then we'll run it. Is that wrong? Well, 4.9 million people thoroughly enjoyed the *News Of The World* last week.'

In fact, it was probably roughly three times that figure:

Piers was quoting circulation figures, not readership levels.

Interestingly, even at this early stage, the fact that he had a brother in the Army gave him some degree of moral authority and, on top of that, he also had a brother-in-law then serving in Bosnia. 'They'd let me know if I'd done the wrong thing,' he insisted – but where, he was asked, would he draw the line?

It turned out that Piers had a humane side after all. He related the story of a BT operator who had chatted up a caller, found out his address and started to stalk him. However, once the *News Of The World* confronted her, she broke down and admitted that she'd just been released from a psychiatric hospital and if they published the story she'd commit suicide. And so they didn't go ahead.

'Morally, I wouldn't have been able to live with myself if she had killed herself,' said Piers.

However, he did run a story in which it emerged that the Bishop of Durham had committed an indecent act in a lavatory, twenty-six years previously. 'I thought very long and hard about it,' said Piers. 'I wasn't happy with the story until we established he had been guilty of hypocrisy. It was obvious the conviction was spent. So we had to ask: should we be pillorying a man for something that had happened so long ago? My immediate answer was that he wasn't a young boy who committed a silly offence. At the time, he was a thirty-one-year-old man, married for five years, doing something quite extraordinary, especially for someone in the Church. What sealed it for me was the fact that he had said quite categorically there was no place in the ministry for gay clergymen.

'OK, twenty-six years is a long time but if he had admitted the offence at his appointment – though I concede it would have been laughable to do so – then I expect people would have said, OK, because it's no longer scandalous to be gay. Instead, he spoke out against gays. Our fourth most senior clergyman was guilty of rank hypocrisy.'

Piers was on a roll – already he had made a splash as editor of 'Bizarre' and now, as editor of the *News Of The World*, he was becoming a name and this thoroughly amused him. And his old school – Chailey – had just been in touch. 'The headmistress has just written to me asking me to open their new science building,' he told *The Spectator*. 'Evidently I'm their most famous old boy. I'll be delighted to do it.'

Another aspect to the job that he hadn't had to address before was politics. As editor of 'Bizarre', Piers had mainly concerned himself with pop stars, but now the country's leaders were getting a look in, too. And so he began to contend with one of the more curious leaps in the difference between his personal beliefs and professional stance, one that would stay with him for years to come: Piers was basically a Tory, who supported Labour and, at that stage, the Conservative Party still ran Britain. Indeed, Tony Blair had only recently been elected Leader of the Labour Party. 'There's no company line and I have an open mind,' said Piers. 'I think Blair is an impressive character. I met him briefly at the Labour Conference and he was a very friendly, likeable chap. [But] yes, I do vote Tory. I'm from true-blue Sussex, I am conservatively oriented and it is my family's way. We had Michael Howard [the then Home Secretary] in recently. We got one of our canteen girls dressed as a jailbird to serve him food – he loved it.'

Murdoch's gamble was paying off and, to celebrate (or at least mark the occasion), Piers gave an interview to the *Independent*. He was, to put it mildly, robust in defence of the stories he'd recently been running, for barely a week had gone by without another scandal in the *News Of The World* setting the pace.

'If they are Tory MPs, and have been elected by preaching family values and use their wife and children in publicity photographs, they deserve to be exposed if they commit adultery,' he declared. 'If, say, David Mellor [the Secretary of State for National Heritage, who was forced to resign after a series of scandals], when he stood for election, had said vote for me and, oh, by the way, I'll frequently be unfaithful to my wife during the time I'm your MP, and they still voted for him, then good luck to him. I'm not personally laying down rules – I'm just saying that the public servants paid for by us have got to be accountable. It's not just politicians. Of course I sympathise with people like Mrs Mellor and her children, but innocent people always suffer when there's any sort of scandal. The *Financial Times* might expose some crooked

City con man, but no one criticises them, though there will be innocent people who suffer.'

However, it was not just politicians and clergymen who featured in the *News Of The World* – just about any celebrity caught out doing what they shouldn't have been doing did so, too. But Piers was prepared to mount a strong defence. 'It is a different agenda with pop stars,' he acknowledged, 'they court newspaper publicity to sell their records, so they have to accept the bad publicity as well. You may think that's a pretty spurious argument. In actual fact, I've had pop stars' representatives begging me to run their sex scandals.'

Despite all this success, his hard work was beginning to take its toll, too. Piers' marriage was to stagger on for many years to come, but now, with his eldest son Spencer still just one, he and Marion embarked on a separation. Piers himself was remarkably unforthcoming on what lay behind the move and steadfastly refused to answer questions (ironic, as he himself conceded, for an editor of the *News Of The World*) and, indeed, the two were to eventually reunite. But it was the first sign that his marriage would not stay the course: pressure of work, marrying too young... it was all to add up.

But Piers was doing so well professionally that nothing else seemed to matter. He was also well aware of the person to whom he owed everything – Kelvin MacKenzie. Indeed, he was quite fulsome in his praise, describing him as 'inspirational' and 'incredible'.

'There are people in key positions around the world who are there because of him,' he proudly declared. 'If that's the only thing he's remembered for, then that's still a hell of an achievement.'

And he drew a lot from his old mentor in terms of management style (not least frowning on all-day drinking), but, while Kelvin could be a terrifying boss, roaring with rage at his hapless lieutenants, Piers was – if not gentle as such – a little easier to deal with. 'I wouldn't say anyone here is terrified of me,' he mused. 'People here enjoy coming to work, but they know that I expect a certain standard and I won't tolerate mistakes. I don't like going out for lunch and things like that. I want to be visible so that, when someone wants a decision taken, I can make it rather than have them wait for me to come back from a freebie lunch. I'm full of respect for the staff here; they took me on as a rookie and helped me learn my trade.'

Of course, one of the reasons why he wanted to maintain a constant presence in the office and was always careful to praise his reporters was because he was still so very young. Despite a hugely successful first year in the job, there were still doubters in the industry, to say nothing of his own staff; many had actually been passed over in favour of him and so they might be forgiven for feeling cautious. It simply made good sense to keep them on side.

'I suppose the age thing was a problem,' Piers admitted to *Business Age* on the anniversary of his starting out in the job. 'There are a lot of older people here but journalism is the one profession where age has never mattered. Whether you're seventeen or seventy-five, as long as you know what you're doing, you get respect. I had to gain respect very quickly, and the only way to do that was to produce great stories. I guess I was lucky because we got those stories, thanks to people who've been here longer than me.'

It was altogether a different tone to the one he had set at 'Bizarre', where it had been all about him: now it was all about the paper. Piers had lost none of his knack for self-publicity (indeed, he never would), but he knew that he needed to present an entirely different persona. In short, he had to grow up – and fast.

'The days of the rampant ego maniac are over,' he declared. 'The nation can breathe again. The staff here were as amazed as I was that I got the job. They'd already had three acting editors in three months, so it was a case of, "Oh, here's another one. When's it all going to stop?" They didn't know me from Adam except that I wrote a column on the *Sun*, which was hardly the normal route to editorship. I wasn't going to come in here and throw my weight around. I said to them, "If you give me your support, I'll do my best for you." I never regretted anything I did on the *Sun*. If people want to remember me for writing a book about Take That or being gunged on the Noel Edmonds' show, that's fine. I had great fun in those days, but the bottom line is I don't miss it.'

Among other things, he was showing a talent to reinvent himself and that was standing him in good stead; he would have to do something similar about a decade later when he lost his job as editor of the *Mirror* in spectacular style, but for now he was displaying a crucial ability to change roles, learn fast, up the odds and still come out winning. And he wasn't just the youngest editor on Fleet Street either, he was also the most-talked about and was producing some of the best stories, too. But he couldn't afford to mess up, even now; some of those stories had been highly controversial and, although he was setting the agenda, along the way he constantly had to defend himself and he was certainly able to do that.

'I fully understand that I'm in a powerful position but my motivation is not to slip up,' he explained. 'It's easy to get carried away in this job and make mistakes that will haunt you for the rest of your career. The main concern I have is that I don't drop a spectacular clanger and we get a big libel case. You're talking about huge sums of money awarded arbitrarily by a jury under this strange libel system we live in, but we have to live by it. A simple error can cost hundreds of thousands of pounds. What I'm saying is that every single thing that appears in the *News Of The World* is my responsibility. The buck stops here and I have to live or die by what we print. If I'm still sitting here in three years' time, I'll be very pleased.'

As it happened, he would be even more delighted at where he was to end up.

Piers had only been in the job for just over a year when he received one of the biggest accolades that his industry could bestow. The now-defunct BBC television programme *What The Papers Say* held annual awards, including one for Scoop Of The Year. At the beginning of 1995, this was extended to Scoops Of The Year because the *News Of The World* had achieved so many of them.

'One of the worst things that can happen to someone who has been getting away with something is for someone to tell the *News Of The World*,' said Russell Davies, who was hosting the event. 'Indeed, its track record has been breathtaking. For those who miss the *News Of The World*, it is responsible for what most of Britain is talking about on Monday morning. During the course of 1994, the *News Of The World* consistently produced front-page stories which set the agenda for the week and left other papers trying to catch up. It was essential reading for millions of people.'

As editor, Piers collected the award but, as usual, he was careful to praise journalists working on the paper. 'I'm delighted the consistently brilliant investigative work of journalists on the *News Of The World* has earned them this award,' was how he put it. However, he was the one at the helm, steering the ship, taking risks, and no one was in any doubt that this was very much his award, too.

The next big scandal to hit the decks was actually courtesy of the *Sunday Mirror*, but, given that Piers himself had been behind so many recent sensations, he was forced to defend this one on a matter of principle. It concerned Rupert Pennant-Rea, the Deputy Governor of the Bank of England. Already a much-married man (he was with his third wife by the time the scandal broke), he had been having an affair with journalist Mary Ellen Synon but eventually called it off after four years in 1994. Incandescent with rage, Mary Ellen (who apparently harboured marital ambitions) told her former lover that she would expose him and so she did, although to extend the tension she took a year to go about it. When the story eventually broke, it was packed full of lurid details about lovemaking in the depths of the hallowed Bank and, shortly after it was published, Pennant-Rea resigned from his post. Unusually, Mary Ellen had not been paid for her story but she certainly got the result she wanted.

Pennant-Rea then announced that he had been driven out of office because the press was intruding on his life, a claim backed by the then Chancellor Kenneth Clarke. Questions were raised as to the morality of it all and this was not mere industry speculation; there were constant fears that a privacy law might be introduced, something that would certainly make any editor's job a good deal more difficult. Almost immediately, however, the press rose up to defend itself: usually at one another's throats, this time they spoke as one.

Piers, as might be expected, was one of the most prominent voices. 'It is absolutely ridiculous for the Chancellor and Mr Pennant-Rea to condemn the tabloids,' he declared. 'He only went after the *Financial Times* cleared half a page for the story. My information is he decided to go because he had been exposed to ridicule in the *FT*. It was a story about a man whose judgement is at the essence of our everyday life. When he took his mistress into the office of [Governor of the Bank of England] Eddie George and bonked her on the desk, he invited his own resignation. I'm amazed he hung on so long. It is the usual effort by the Establishment to turn attention on the tabloids, which had very little to do with it.'

In fact, Britain's libel laws are far more draconian than they are in other countries and, in the mid-1990s, there were real concerns that a privacy law might be brought in. Although much of the drama surrounding the royal family was created – and leaked to the press – by the principal members themselves, the public was not so aware of it as they are today. Often journalistic intrusion in those days was condemned by those who didn't realise the press was being used in the 'War of the Waleses'. On the other hand, a dying and weak Conservative Government was filled with politicians with a vested interest in keeping their private lives out of the public eye.

When the then Prime Minister John Major announced it was 'Back to Basics' (in the full knowledge that his own affair with former Conservative minister Edwina Currie could come out at any time) and his 'Minister for Fun' David Mellor announced the press was drinking in the 'Last Chance Saloon', it was open season on anyone with anything to hide. At the same time, the charge was also levelled that newspapers, tabloids in particular, had too much power and should not be allowed to hound people out of office. Altogether, it was an uneasy time.

Stories such as Pennant-Rea's were a case in point: was there really any public interest in exposing his affair (although it should be noted that it was his erstwhile mistress who shopped him, not some snooping tabloid hack) and should he be forced to step down? In truth, he had become a figure of fun and so his fate was almost certainly unavoidable, but it was a real concern for editors of the day.

In March 1995, Piers turned thirty and was still the youngest editor at the table. The scoops continued to roll in: the latest to feature was the Conservative MP Richard Spring, Parliamentary Private Secretary to Sir Patrick Mayhew, the Secretary of State for Northern Ireland. Spring, it emerged, had enjoyed a 'three-in-a-bed sex romp' with a Sunday school teacher and another male friend. It made the front page of the *News Of The World*, and afterwards Spring duly resigned, which again raised eyebrows. After all, he was divorced, on top of which Odette Nightingale – the teacher in question – attended the 'sex romp' with a tape recorder in tow. 'Entrapment is an ugly word,' thundered some sections of the media, leaping to the high moral ground and, indeed, in this case, it did look as if the paper might have gone too far.

'That anyone is entitled to privacy in their homes, in their cups or in their beds is a concept wholly alien to the *News Of The World*,' boomed Lord Wyatt of Weeford in

The Times. 'The *News Of The World* has as good as asked for a privacy law. The Government and Opposition should no longer hesitate to produce it.'

The attack was a little odd, coming as it did not only from a fellow journalist but also one with a column on the *News Of The World*, writing under the moniker 'The Voice Of Reason'.

Another former *News Of The World* reporter who didn't wish to be named (it wasn't a good idea to fall foul of Rupert Murdoch) was equally scathing. 'Patsy [the former editor] would never have run the story on Spring,' he declared. 'Where's the justification? He's a single man, who's been set up in his own home by a woman who's getting a lot of money from the paper. I'm not saying we never put tape recorders under beds but they were a precaution in case we were sued. We've now got inexperienced journalists and an inexperienced editor leading us straight to a privacy law.'

Ultimately, it didn't prove to be the case and, besides, such criticism was more often than not a case of sour grapes. Piers, as was so frequently pointed out, was young – younger than many of his staff and younger than most of Fleet Street – and yet he had already risen to a powerful position. This was bound to engender envy, and any mistakes (and in retrospect this might apply to the Spring story) were bound to be leapt on.

And then there was another aspect to the whole thing: the fact that broadsheets liked to denounce the antics of the tabloids while slavering over the details themselves. 'What we are seeing yet again is double-edged hypocrisy, all the broadsheets splashing on our story on Monday and filling their boots with the salacious details they so condemn,' snapped Piers. 'And then saying how awful it was we ran the story in the first place but giving it wider currency, all the same.'

So who was right? Over a decade and a half later, there is still no privacy law in Britain – and Piers Morgan has certainly become one of the country's best-known names.

CHAPTER FOUR

MAN IN THE MIRROR

I t was just over a year since he'd taken the editor's chair at the *News Of The World* and, whatever anyone might think of him personally, Piers Morgan had certainly turned his paper into a talking point. While the critics and colleagues continued to squabble over what should make the pages of a newspaper, his circulation figures spoke for themselves. In his first year, circulation was up 1.6 per cent. Clearly, the readership approved of what he was doing, even if there was caution elsewhere. And the plaudits were flooding in: Editor of the Year, Newspaper of the Year and Scoop(s) of the Year.

But Piers showed no sign of letting up. Another couple in the news at that time were Charles Spencer (Princess Diana's brother) and his then wife, Victoria. They were about to separate, and Victoria, a former model, was known to have had all sorts of past travails with drink and drugs. She was now being treated for an eating disorder and the *News Of The World* pictured her at a clinic where she was receiving treatment, leading the intemperate Earl Spencer to dub the tabloid press 'hypocritical and evil'. Back then, no one knew that he was repeatedly unfaithful to his wife and would go on to develop quite a reputation because of the way he treated women.

The couple were separating after six years of marriage and, because Charles was Diana's brother, there was intense interest in their every move. People would sell stories about them, and so, to test one particular acquaintance under suspicion, Lord Spencer informed him that he was leaving to work at a television station in New York. The story duly made its way into the press, specifically the front page of the *News Of The World*, whereupon Spencer gleefully rang the paper and told reporters they had been fooled. He had actually written a letter to the person in question, claiming that he and his four children were relocating to New York to see what happened, and was delighted when the entirely false news was printed in full.

'Over the past few weeks it has become apparent to my wife and I that we have a friend who has been informing the *News Of The World*,' a vindicated Spencer told the Press Association. 'To find out who this was, we decided to release false information to the main suspect. My wife and I are both sorry that he has sought to gain from the *News Of The World* rather than respect his friendship with my wife. He was able, with his boyfriend, to take hospitality repeatedly over the past few years and has repaid us in this shabby way. I am delighted we have found out who it was, but I am saddened for my wife that one of her closest friends has turned out to be a traitor. I don't take any pleasure in trying to catch people out like this.'

As soon as the first edition of the paper appeared, the *News Of The World* was alerted and hastily moved the story back to page 13. Naturally, this was a highly embarrassing episode and, clearly ruffled, Piers sought to play down the damage. The newspaper had published the story 'in good faith' he said, before adding, 'I am extremely surprised that Lord Spencer should involve his ailing wife and his children in such an elaborate attempt to deceive a newspaper. He has also quite deliberately attracted a whole new avalanche of publicity at a time when he himself has repeatedly pleaded for privacy on behalf of Lady Victoria.'

There was history here: six months after Lord Spencer married Victoria, he had a brief fling with a former girlfriend – cartoonist Sally Ann Lasson – the news of which duly appeared in the *News Of The World*. That had been before Piers' time, but Spencer had obviously neither forgiven nor forgotten. Not only was it embarrassing, it was bad timing, too. The general feeling was that Piers was pushing it to the limits at the *News Of The World*, running stories that could barely be said to be in the public interest and shining a highly unfavourable light on the industry as a whole. And then, to make matters worse, he was held to account by the Press Complaints Commission and publicly rebuked by his proprietor, Rupert Murdoch.

The cause of all this was, again, Lord Spencer; he was livid when pictures of Victoria, believed to be suffering from bulimia, attending a private clinic in Surrey had appeared. It was also thought she might have a continuing problem with drink. Lord Spencer complained, successfully, to the PCC; they upheld his complaint and the PCC's chairman Lord Wakeham sent a personal letter to Murdoch to bring the matter to his attention, something only done in 'severe or calculated' breaches of the newspaper Code of Practice.

Rupert Murdoch was a complicated figure himself. For a start, there was a certain amount of controversy that one person, who was not even British, could own such a huge chunk of the British media – five newspapers (at times) and a large part of a television station, BSkyB. Second, it was often averred that his newspapers had a Republican agenda; Murdoch himself was a Republican, no doubt about that, but for his publications to have taken such a stance would have caused huge controversy – and this was a story with a royal connection. Third, there was still the issue about a privacy law and Murdoch did not want to see one of his papers blamed for bringing it in, and so he acted quickly.

Piers Morgan 'had gone over the top', he said in a statement. 'This company will not tolerate its papers bringing into disrepute the best practices of popular journalism, which we seek to follow. While I will always support worthwhile investigative journalism as a community responsibility, it is clear that the young man went over the top. Mr Morgan has assured me that his forthcoming apology to Countess Spencer on this matter is severe and without reservation. I have no hesitation in making public this remonstration and I have reminded Mr Morgan forcefully of his responsibility to the Code to which he as editor – and all our journalists – subscribe in their terms of employment.'

For Piers, this was a serious and very public humiliation. The emphasis on youth could not have gone down well and it also emerged that wiser counsel within the newspaper had urged him not to publish the picture. He had ignored that sage advice and now found himself publicly brought to book. Piers had ruffled more than a few feathers in the course of his climb up the greasy pole and, as someone who not only set the news agenda for the past 15 months or so, but had also won a handful of awards for doing so, he was unaccustomed to being rapped over the knuckles so publicly, like a naughty schoolboy. The gloating from other quarters that accompanied it didn't go down well, either.

'I think Mr Murdoch is to be congratulated for taking such a strong line,' said a clearly pleased Lord Wakeham. 'I think papers are taking the Code increasingly seriously.' He went on to announce that the PCC had considered looking into the story involving Richard Spring, but could take no action because Spring understandably wanted to let the matter drop and had therefore not issued a formal complaint.

'While the commission is unable to make a judgment on this case, it also raises questions about the manner in which the *News of the World* has recently applied the public interest criteria of the Code,' he stated.

And Piers appeared duly chastened. 'The decision to publish the story and the photograph of Countess Spencer was mine, and mine alone,' he insisted. 'I am sending my sincere apologies to the Countess for any distress that our actions may have caused at an obviously difficult time for her. Mr Murdoch has made his feelings on this subject very clear to me.'

This was a quite different take from what appeared in the *News Of The World* after Spencer first made his complaint. There, over a full page devoted to the story, was the headline HYPOCRISY OF THE ARROGANT EARL SPENCER ... HIS PRIVACY CAN BE INVADED FOR CASH, after which followed a list of the various occasions on which Spencer had given exclusives to magazines such as *Hello!*.

The PCC was not impressed. 'While this affects the extent to which he may now be entitled to privacy in respect of particular aspects of his own life, we do not believe that this leaves the press free to report on any matter regarding the Countess,' it stated.

To make matters worse, Piers was then threatened with being sent to prison, albeit on the back of yet another crisis. The reason was a *News Of The World* exclusive exposing a drugs dealer, complete with his name, age, occupation and the town where he lived; the problem was that the dealer was, in fact, awaiting trial for criminal charges, and the piece was therefore in contempt of court – his details should never have been published. So, could matters get any worse? It seemed they could.

Piers was now truly having to take on board Kelvin MacKenzie's contention that, if an editor was prepared to dish it out, he should also be able to take it in a big way; he was accustomed to training a lens on the love lives of the big names of the day but rather less used to having the tables turned. He had publicly admitted that he was separated from his wife and, until June 1995, a few weeks after he'd been chastised by Murdoch, that had been that, but then a bizarre story emerged, linking him with a woman called Sheryl Kyle, now rather better known as Sheryl Gascoigne. Back then, she was Paul Gascoigne's on-off girlfriend and would later become his wife. Piers was unavailable for comment to the *London Evening Standard*'s 'Londoner's Diary' where the story first appeared and the newspaper had to content itself with a comment from his mother.

'I expect mums are the last to know,' Gabrielle cheerfully observed.

Max Clifford also managed to get himself involved, announcing, 'Piers and Sheryl were making a record together.'

With all the criticism he was receiving from every side, Piers refused to take it on the chin and flew into a rage. Just a day later, the 'Londoner's Diary' printed a retraction, telling readers that Piers was furious – as the story was altogether untrue, especially the part about his making an album – and relaying that he had told them the news would upset his estranged wife and they'd had no business contacting his family. It might have seemed a bit rich, coming from the editor of the *News of the World*, but Piers was clearly fed up. Sheryl, too, confirmed that there was no truth in the story whatsoever.

Meanwhile, he was attempting to get on with business as usual, which that week involved buying up the story of Divine Brown, the prostitute who had recently been arrested alongside actor Hugh Grant, thus blowing out of the water Grant's persona as the ultimate English gentleman. The *News Of The World*'s rival paper, the *People*, then accused Piers of chequebook journalism, something he hotly denied. 'What happened is that our reporter was on a Los Angeles TV show and was asked what he thought the story could be worth,' he explained. 'He speculated that it could be worth up to $100,000 or so, but we didn't pay anything like that – it was not money that got the story, it was the speed at which we got to her. We used brilliant investigative journalism techniques to track her down.'

This wasn't what he was used to, though: Piers had been doing so well for so long that to have people accuse him of entrapment (Richard Spring), intruding on the privacy of a sick woman (Victoria Spencer) and now using a fat chequebook rather than investigative techniques to land that week's scoop must have been galling. He was more accustomed to being the Boy Wonder, not someone publicly chastised by Rupert Murdoch for bringing the profession into disrepute. Naturally, he wasn't enjoying his editorship one jot at this stage.

People were beginning to tease him about recent events, too. When it was revealed that Sheryl Kyle was pregnant with Paul Gascoigne's child, the *Guardian*'s diarist rang to ask him to congratulate the happy couple. Piers didn't call back, although he did so the very next day.

'The *Daily Mail* has confronted Gazza with the fact that I'm the father,' he said. 'But look, I've only met Sheryl twice in my life. It's so preposterous that I'm finding it quite funny [but] Gazza's in a terrible state. It's splendid that the papers want to delve into my private life, but they really should leave him alone. Listen, if the baby was mine, don't you think I'd be the first to buy myself up?'

It was all stated in as joking a fashion as he could manage (and this was far from the last time that rival newspapers would take an in-depth look at his personal life), but Piers had clearly come under a great deal of pressure: to go from *wunderkind* to whipping boy was not a pleasurable experience. There was an increasing sense that something had to give, and so it did.

The news broke towards the end of August 1995: Piers Morgan had resigned from the *News Of The World* and was to edit the *Daily Mirror* instead. Again, the hand of Kelvin MacKenzie could clearly be seen to be moving behind the scenes; after a brief spell at BSkyB, he himself had moved to the Mirror Group, where he was running the television interests. He would have understood just how humiliating Piers found it to be so publicly ticked off and he also knew that his protégé, while a maverick, was brilliant at getting scoops and attracting publicity, both for himself and his papers.

And so the deal was struck: the current editor of the *Mirror* – Colin Myler – became managing editor of both the *Daily* and *Sunday Mirror*, a management role rather than an editorial one, and the Boy Wonder signed up to the team. 'I have been offered the editorship of the *Daily Mirror* and I have accepted,' announced Piers in a somewhat chilly statement. 'I have given in my notice.'

At this, Rupert Murdoch was livid: just a couple of months earlier, he'd been slapping Piers Morgan down and now here was his editor doing pretty much the same in return. Initially, it seemed as if he would try to force him to stay – after all, he had between a year and eighteen months left on his contract and it seemed News International was in no mood to release him.

'Piers Morgan remains the editor of the *News Of The World* under the terms of the contract,' was the stiff statement from the company. But it was no good; his heart was no longer in it and Piers wanted out. The *Mirror* executives themselves were determined to get their man; they announced that Myler would continue to edit the paper until he was able to take up the appointment. Clearly, it was just a matter of time.

Meanwhile, over at the *Mirror*, there were concerns among the staff on the ground, too. Piers had spent most of his professional life on the *Sun* and the *News Of The World*, both Conservative supporters. The *Mirror*, on the other hand, was Labour through and through. Previously, he had also admitted to voting Tory and his new staff expressed alarm that he might try to impose his views on them.

'The big fear is for the left-wing leanings on the paper,' revealed one journalist, who refused to be named. 'There must also be worries that we'll be going downmarket with more kiss-and-tell stories. Although we're a tabloid at the lower end of the market, we've always managed to cover the serious news in a way our readers would understand.'

But there was no backing out: Piers was on his way. Then came another slew of headlines about his youth because, at the tender age of thirty, he would now become the youngest editor of a daily newspaper. At the same time, the *News Of The World* finally accepted the fact that he was leaving and appointed the paper's deputy (Phil Hall) as editor in his place.

In the event, Piers became editor of the *Mirror* less than two months after he tendered his resignation from the *News Of The World* and lost no time in making his presence felt. And, while he made it clear that he would deliver a serious news agenda, he also had that extra sense so crucial to any editor to know exactly what his readership was really interested in. And so, in November 1995, when Diana,

Princess of Wales did a completely unprecedented and, at that time, extremely shocking interview with Martin Bashir on BBC's *Panorama*, he pulled out all the stops. Here was the Princess of Wales talking about the 'three of us in the marriage, so it was a little crowded', asserting she wanted to be 'the Queen of People's Hearts' and saying that Prince Charles shouldn't become king. The appearance caused a complete sensation, made divorce from Charles inevitable – at the time they were only separated – and was front-page news for almost every newspaper.

The *Mirror* really went to town; the next day, sixteen pages were set aside for news (as opposed to features, columns, sport and so on) and every single one was devoted to the Diana interview. Piers himself declared it to be the biggest story he had ever reported and said the blanket coverage was completely unprecedented – it certainly was that.

Indeed, he came in for a lot of stick for making that particular issue of the paper, the 'Diana' issue (before numerous 'Diana' issues in the wake of her death), but the fact is he was right. When he joined the *Mirror*, it had lost its identity to a certain extent. Once a solid, working-class newspaper, the readership it used to represent was no longer the same. Margaret Thatcher had made large sections of the working class considerably better off; it was no good assuming 'working class' automatically meant 'left wing', and the paper no longer seemed to know who it should appeal to. For the years preceding Piers' arrival, it appeared to position itself as a left-wing version of the *Sun*, but that didn't work either. And so he started to give the paper a desperately needed shot in the arm.

The fact is that at the time everyone in Britain was obsessed with Princess Diana and, increasingly, with celebrity, too. But Piers was savvy enough to realise he could combine that enthusiasm with the paper's left-leaning political stance and make it a lively journal of its own. It was only towards the very end of his tenure that he began to misjudge his readership, mainly by failing to support British soldiers in Iraq. For the best part of the next decade, he was to make the *Mirror* a serious player on the block.

As ever, his timing was spot on: a month or so after he stepped into the editor's chair at the *Mirror*, another mid-market tabloid owned by Rupert Murdoch (*Today*) closed. Its readers had to go somewhere and, for a fair few of them, that outlet was the *Mirror*. At the same time, the *Mirror* also picked up some of the more experienced *Today* staff. One was the *Today* features editor Tina Weaver. In 2001, she became editor of the *Sunday Mirror*, a mark of the quality of staff coming on board.

Meanwhile, Piers was proving his doubters wrong by putting in fifteen-hour days, roaring around the office and shaking the place from head to foot. 'It's great fun,' he told the UK *Press Gazette*. 'I have inherited a brilliant team of journalists. I was a writer myself and I know how egos have to be pandered to. The *Mirror* is a great institution and they are a great team, raring for battle.'

That appreciation cut both ways: journalists were really beginning to warm to him.

Piers had the ability to take the political adjustment on board, too. Far from imposing right-wing ideas on a paper that would have been hard-pressed to accept them, he was somehow at one with the mood of the country. The Conservative Government, led by John Major, was in its dying embers and Britain was desperate for change. The country was beginning to fall in love with Tony Blair and New Labour, and Piers was there to guide them as they did so.

'I never had particularly strong feelings [about politics] either way,' he told *Campaign*. 'This time I do – I do feel this Government has let down the country. One of the reasons I came to the *Mirror* when I did was the impending election. We hadn't had the *Daily Mirror* supporting a Labour Government for a very long time and I think it will have a very positive effect on sales.'

Indeed, he lost no time in giving his latest newspaper a makeover. He started to pursue a far more serious news agenda than previously, and hired a slew of new writers, including Jo Brand, Victor Lewis-Smith and Tony Parsons, who, at the time of writing, still has his own column. But he also trusted his instincts, which meant a huge focus on the National Lottery and, of course, the royals. Diana, in particular, could make the front pages just by changing her outfit and was still one of the most potent selling weapons any paper has ever had at its disposal. And that *Panorama* interview simply made the whole story more gripping still. Recently, Diana had been cornered in the street by some paparazzi who goaded her so much that she finally broke down in tears – pictures that the *Mirror* ran, and for which they were heavily criticised.

Meanwhile, Piers was having none of it. 'Some people are sick and tired of reading about them [the royals], but a lot of people are still fascinated,' he told the *Guardian*. 'The broadsheets have been running reams on it too, because it's a constitutional issue. In the case of Princess Di, it would be pretty hard for her to expect too much privacy, given that she went on television to spill the beans about her private life. I'm sure she weighed up the significance of that, and realised that her continual protestations of privacy would have a hollow ring.

'Everyone got worked up about that video showing the paparazzi behaving badly. I could never have condoned that behaviour but nor am I going to join the ranks of newspaper critics. The photographers were caught by surprise when Diana began to run and they ran after her. I firmly believe that her breaking down in the street had nothing to do with that – that's why we took the decision to publish the picture of her crying. I felt it was indicative of her state of mind and it was a pretty powerful image.'

Of course, just eighteen months later, Princess Diana was to die after the car in which she was travelling with her then boyfriend Dodi Fayed was forced to escape a paparazzi in hot pursuit, but no one yet realised quite how much she was having to suffer from the rogue element.

It had been a controversial decision, though: over at the *Sun*, the pictures did not appear in the paper, and its editor pointed out that Diana should really have some form of protection whenever she went out. Piers remained as pragmatic as ever. 'We're all beginning to ask whether there's royal overkill but the circulation figures suggest otherwise,' he declared.

He was determined to maintain his credentials as a serious editor, too. The British Government had recently announced a knife amnesty, as a result of which 40,000 weapons had been handed in. Piers decided the *Mirror* should support the campaign and produced a front page with a picture of a man's head with a knife sticking out of it.

'I felt it was the most powerful image to back the campaign,' he explained. 'We were given the picture by this man and encouraged by him to use it. The idea that you could have a knife through the back of your head and survive was astonishing. Sales were pretty good on that day. We had some strong reactions and I published them in a letters special.'

Other antics at the time included branding the then Home Office minister Ann Widdecombe 'Doris Karloff' – a nickname that stuck for years.

Piers' new-style *Mirror* was certainly making an impact, something gracefully conceded by his biggest rival. Stuart Higgins was editor of the *Sun*, which had a higher circulation and was the more successful of the two newspapers, but he did agree that the new editor over at the *Mirror* was making a difference. 'The paper looks a lot sharper, a lot livelier and more energetic, a lot of ideas going into it and it's giving us some healthy competition for a change,' he observed. 'We've raised our game to compete. What the *Mirror* still lacks is the humour that was unique to the *Sun*. No matter how hard it tries to copy the *Sun*, it can't recreate the humour. Its one advantage is the strong disillusion with the Tory Government. If there is a change of government, the *Daily Mirror*'s fortunes may change.'

Piers' youth remained an issue – indeed, so much has been made of it that, even now, in his mid-forties, he is still viewed as a very young man – but the Boy Wonder had a few older hands keeping an eye on things, too. Kelvin MacKenzie, while not exactly hovering over his shoulder, was certainly looking up from his desk where he managed the *Mirror*'s television interests to give the odd word of advice, as were other seasoned industry professionals, including Charlie Wilson (then acting editor of the *Independent*, a stable-mate) and David Montgomery, chief executive of Mirror Group.

Indeed, Montgomery was widely believed to be responsible for spiking a story that would have been vintage Piers: Morgan had been on the verge of buying up the tale of Darius Guppy, as related by the man himself.

Guppy and Earl Spencer had been each other's best man (although they were to fall out spectacularly years later when Darius discovered that Spencer had made a pass at his own wife, something which the Earl denies), but Guppy had been convicted of a £1.8 million insurance fraud and got out of jail in early 1996. Piers wanted to run his take on what had happened to him, but it's thought Montgomery skewered the deal as it contravened the newspaper Code of Practice, which forbids a convicted criminal from profiting by selling a story. The Countess Spencer fiasco had not been so long ago and clearly all concerned were determined no similar breach of the Code would take place at the *Mirror*. In public at least, Piers toed the party line. 'The *Daily Mirror* has an absolute policy of not paying money to convicted criminals,' he insisted.

On that occasion, Piers might have been saved from himself, but, in June 1996, he went too far once more; the World Cup was on and England were playing Germany, always a potent combination. Of course, the tabloids rose to the challenge: the *Sun*'s headline read: LET'S BLITZ FRITZ, while the *Daily Star* ran a picture of England coach Terry Venables in the style of the famous poster 'Your Country Needs You'.

But Piers went much, much further. His headline was ACHTUNG! SURRENDER, followed by: 'For you, Fritz, the Euro 96 Championship is over'. Inside, it got worse. Another headline read: MIRROR DECLARES FOOTBALL WAR ON GERMANY over a pastiche of Neville Chamberlain's 1939 speech declaring the outbreak of World War II: 'Last night the *Daily Mirror*'s Ambassador in Berlin handed the German Government a final note stating that, unless we heard from them by 11 o'clock that they were prepared at once to withdraw their team from Wembley, a state of soccer war would exist between us. I have to tell you that no such undertaking has been received. Against these evils, I am certain that inside right will prevail.' All this was illustrated with doctored photos of Paul Gascoigne and Stuart Pearce wearing army helmets and a subheading read: PEARCE IN OUR TIME.

Other headlines included: WHO DO YOU THINK YOU ARE KIDDING MR HITMAN? and VE ARE NOT FOOLED, FRITZ. Reporter Justin Dunn was then despatched to Berlin. 'There is a strange smell in Berlin and it's not just their funny sausages,' he wrote. 'It's the smell of fear, because deep down, they know we're going to beat them again.' And so it went on.

The resulting outrage was massive and immediate: the Press Complaints Commission was swamped with calls, as was the *Mirror*. Sir Bobby Charlton, no less, was none too happy. 'I really wish they would think before they put all this in print,' he said. 'It's a very difficult thing. It does create hatred, which in 99 per cent of the people is not there.'

Terry Venables was equally unimpressed. 'It is not just an insult to the Germans, it is an insult to the intelligence of the English people and those who have fought for their country within wars,' he observed. 'At the end of the day, it is football, not war. I just hope the fans understand that.'

The German side didn't issue a statement (indeed, it was unnecessary, given how almost everyone was outraged on their behalf), but the German Ambassador in London did object. 'Sport should not be connected with a war which, for the Germans, is a very strong reminder of a past they do not care to brag about,' he said.

Meanwhile, horrified *Mirror* executives came down on Piers like a tonne of bricks and forced him to issue an apology, but he himself showed every indication of simply not understanding the extent of the furore he had caused. 'We just want people to have a bit of fun, a bit of humour,' he protested. 'Humour about the Germans has gone back in our history and is reflected in programmes like *Dad's Army* and *'Allo 'Allo*. It was intended as a joke, but anyone who was offended by it must have taken it seriously and, to those people, I say sorry.'

But it could have been a whole lot worse: there were rumours that Piers (or one of his lieutenants) had planned to drive a tank into Germany, that the paper had been arranging a Spitfire flypast over the London hotel in which the German team was staying and that he'd looked into reuniting the cast of *Dad's Army*. Then again, it could have been a whole lot better. But the *Mirror* had wanted an editor capable of causing the nation to choke on its morning cuppa – sometimes at the sheer brilliance of the scoop and sometimes at the sheer scale of the misjudgement – and that's what it got. Besides, everyone had been warned: they knew their man had been given a public carpeting by Rupert Murdoch, which is why they'd managed to lure him away in the first place. What's more, they were keen to keep him (say what you like, everyone was certainly talking about the *Mirror*) and so the matter was dropped.

It was the first massively controversial front page that Piers had created for his new paper... and it certainly wasn't to be the last.

CHAPTER FIVE

THE DEATH
OF DIANA

Piers had apologised, but the ACHTUNG! SURRENDER furore took some time to calm down. After all, this was the second time in less than a year that he had made a serious miscalculation and, while a maverick but brilliant young editor might get away with a certain amount, another mistake on this scale could be seriously damaging. More than sixty complaints had been lodged with the Press Complaints Commission, while widespread condemnation continued. Piers did what he could to calm everyone down: the next day's paper showed the German captain Jürgen Klinsmann accepting a Harrods' hamper as a peace offering, under the headline PEAS IN OUR TIME.

Certainly, everyone was having a lot of fun with puns. Over at the *Sun*, there was talk of 'appiersment', while the Boy Wonder had also been dubbed Piers 'Guten' Morgan. Rather more seriously, a couple of advertisers pulled their campaigns from the *Mirror* (not the best development for a paper with a falling circulation), at which point the Mirror Group's share price slipped a couple of points. Far much more seriously, Germany then beat England on penalties, which led to rioting in the streets afterwards. In this unwelcome development, Piers was openly blamed for winding people up. Comedienne and columnist Jo Brand, meanwhile, let it be known that she wouldn't be renewing her contract. Apparently, she too disapproved of the paper's stance.

Some predicted this would be the end of Piers' reign, but they were totally wrong. It wasn't long before he had tuned into what the readers wanted and launched a campaign to force the royal family to give Princess Diana back her title. She had lost 'HRH' following her divorce from Prince Charles in 1996, although at this stage it wasn't quite finalised and, in the wake of this, withdrew from her position as patron of over a hundred charities. Following this, the *Mirror* launched not only a legal challenge but also a petition to reverse the move.

'The decision to remove the title Her Royal Highness from the Princess of Wales by Buckingham Palace has become a matter of enormous public interest,' Piers declared. 'The *Daily Mirror* believes that the removal of the title is damaging to the public interest and goes against public opinion. We feel it is now imperative that the Court should reconsider the full implications before granting a Decree Absolute.'

It proved a clever move; Princess Diana, with whom

Piers had recently lunched, was still enormously popular and the newspaper could do no wrong in issuing messages of public support for her. Nor did it hurt that it rather deflected attention from the unfortunate ACHTUNG! SURRENDER front page.

In the background, Piers and Marion decided to give their marriage another go and their next child, Stanley Christopher, was born in 1997. However, the reunion was not to last. One problem, according to friends, was that Marion sometimes seemed to put her husband down in public, always eager to assert that her career as a nurse was just as important as Piers' life as a newspaper editor. But, while this might have been true, she was nothing like as high profile as her husband, which perhaps jarred. Either way, she did not appear to be offering him the support he wished for and many were not surprised when the marriage eventually fell apart.

Diana provided more useful diversionary tactics when a fake video of her cavorting half-naked with James Hewitt came to light – in fact, the couple on screen were actors. The *Sun* got hold of the story, believed the video to be real and put it on the front page, at which point it was promptly proved to be a fake. Piers was merciless; he gave up pages one to seven of his own paper to gloat over the *Sun*'s distress: HOAX OF THE CENTURY – HOW THE SUN WAS SUCKERED was the main headline. It was a welcome opportunity to point the finger at another editor who had messed up – and his greatest rival at that. What's more,

Piers happily appeared on the BBC to hammer the point home. It emerged the video had, in fact, first been offered to three other publications: *Here!* magazine in the UK, plus the *Star* and *Globe* in the States.

Indeed, Piers seemed so pleased about it that some people even began to speculate that the *Mirror* itself was behind the hoax, something he was forced to hotly deny. 'We did not engineer the hoax,' he insisted. 'Hand on heart, the first we knew about this was midday yesterday when Max Clifford called me, acting on behalf of the director of the video, Nick Hedges. I was here on the night the story dropped and it was a very long night indeed when I thought we'd been regally scooped. It was quite clear when we saw the video this was exactly how the scam operated.

'I have no idea how a copy came to be offered to the *Sun*; I do know it was offered to other media operations first. Clearly, somebody was trying to con the papers. Can you imagine any national newspaper deliberately trying to stitch up another with a fake video? I'm sure he'll [*Sun* editor Stuart Higgins] feel pretty peeved about it, but at the end of the day he was hoaxed, and I would be as keen to find out who did that as anybody else.'

He also felt there was no need for Higgins to lose his job – and, given how often he himself had recently been skating on thin ice, it should have come as no surprise when he took that line – and, with that, it was business as normal.

No one had ever quite got to the root of the stories about Piers and Sheryl Gascoigne, as she now was, but the paper maintained a remarkably sympathetic stance towards her. She and Paul had been married in mid-1996 and, barely three months later, she was pictured in the *Mirror* with a bruised face and her arm in a sling. The headline read: GAZZA BEATS SHERYL BLACK AND BLUE and was followed by the full story of how he'd flown into a drunken rage at his new wife. Allegations continued to fly that Piers and Sheryl were on closer terms than might have previously been thought, but this was untrue – after all, he was now trying to make a go of it with Marion again. But it did show that his news sense was still second to none.

That news sense – and signs of a more mature Piers – surfaced once more in the autumn of 1996, when a bundle of papers was handed in to the *Mirror*. The documents were found to contain extremely sensitive information about the forthcoming Budget, but rather than publish them, as he might have done a year or so previously, Piers handed them in to Number 10. It was a win-win situation: he had a huge story on his hands anyway with the leak of the information, while at the same time he came across as responsible and praiseworthy for handing the documents back without revealing their contents.

'Although we wouldn't normally hesitate to embarrass the Government with such an amazing scoop, on this occasion we had a public duty to return such sensitive economic documents,' he said. 'Publication of so much detail from the Budget before the Chancellor's speech could have forced the stock market to close and cause chaos in the international money markets. These were in the main press releases, which would be issued at the end of the speech on every individual point. I think it would be fairly obvious why they chose the *Mirror*: if you are going to embarrass the Government, then we are the perfect receptacle.'

Except this time round, they weren't. Piers had had to put up with a lot of criticism since taking up the mantle of editor on the grounds that he was a pop-music critic, not a serious journalist, and also on the basis that he was a Tory and therefore not the obvious choice for the left-leaning *Mirror*, but this latest episode showed that he was well aware of the political impact the leaked documents might have had, and to do anything else with them would have been irresponsible. He chose by far the best course of action and, as a result, his standing rose.

It was certainly an embarrassment for the British Government. Prime Minister John Major ordered an immediate inquiry. 'We are grateful for them having returned the papers,' said a spokesman. 'It would have been against the public interest for there to be premature publication.'

From intemperate risk-taker just a couple of months earlier, Piers had now donned the mantle of responsible member of the press, and was thoroughly enjoying being on the side of good for a change. Not that he was allowed to revel in it for long, as the rest of Fleet Street rounded on him, saying they would have published the information and condemned him for loss of nerve. Indeed, it was soon doing the rounds that the real reason why Piers didn't publish was because he thought it could be an elaborate hoax and, after his recent difficulties, to say nothing of witnessing first hand the *Sun*'s humiliation, he simply wasn't about to chance it.

While Piers was adamant he was just being responsible, others weren't quite so sure, but he conceded that, given his past record, he had to be extremely careful. 'If I had published them and they turned out to be a hoax, I would have been sacked the next morning,' he admitted. 'And I was very hoax-minded, given what happened to the *Sun* over the fake tape of Diana and Hewitt.'

As all this was going on, he was beginning to take steps in another direction: appearing on TV. Still only thirty-one, he was one of the best-known editors in the country and was clearly thinking along the lines of becoming a media personality as well, but his initial forays were unsuccessful. Towards the end of 1996, he appeared on Paul Merton's team in the BBC comedy quiz programme *Have I Got News For You*. This backfired disastrously: totally misjudging the mood of the audience, he attempted to rally them on his side against Ian Hislop, only for the audience to roar in support of the *Private Eye* editor.

'Does anybody actually like him?' he demanded of the audience, to which they all cried back, '*Yes!*'

Piers knew it had been a disaster and initially could

get very cool with anyone who brought up the subject. It looked as if his putative TV career was over before it had begun. In time, however, he learned to take it on the chin; given that television was the medium in which he would one day become a household name, this was, in fact, an invaluable experience, even if it didn't feel like it at the time and so Piers was eventually able to mock himself.

The following year, he proclaimed, 'I hugely enjoyed my own embarrassment and humiliation, and was confused that people didn't realise that.' But it had taken a while. 'After the fourteenth video rerun at Christmas, even I began to see that my magical wit lacked a certain brilliance on the evening, though I deluded myself at the time,' he went on. 'I would advise anybody in the same position to be prepared for the flak if your jokes go flat, but it is better to go on than not. Don't go expecting people to find you hugely amusing. Even if you are that funny, I'm sure the best bits are taken out to make themselves look better.'

Back at the *Mirror*, at this stage, he was now in an unusual position: he was criticised when he ran a sensitive story, but criticised when he decided against doing so. Of course, a lot of this came down to resentment. Even his biggest fans would have to concede that Piers could come across as bumptious: a combination of arrogance and hard work had taken him to the top of the tree when he was still very young, but that meant his rivals felt little compunction in knocking him down.

In some ways, he was a victim of his own success; the

A young, fresh-faced Piers in his showbiz reporting days with, *above*, Take That and, *below*, Dannii Minogue.

With his first wife, Marion, at Marco Pierre White's wedding in 2000.

As Editor of the *Mirror*, Piers was often the subject of media attention himself. He is pictured *below* outside the High Court after the newspaper lost the case brought against it by Naomi Campbell.

Keep your friends close … Piers with the manager of his beloved Arsenal, Arsène Wenger (*above*) …but keep your enemies closer … Piers and Jeremy Clarkson have had a media-driven feud for a number of years (*below*).

Mixing with the political heavyweights. *Above*: With Nelson Mandela and, *below*, at the Pride of Britain Awards with Tony and Cherie Blair. Piers later admitted that there was no love lost between himself and Cherie.

A different kind of editorship – the launch of *First News*, written by adults for children. Piers is Editorial Director of the newspaper.

Above: Piers with the editor of *First News*, Nicky Cox, and the members of operatic pop group G4.

Below: Taking a look at his new creation with, *left*, former Prime Minister Gordon Brown and, *right*, Kevin Pietersen.

Keeping on top of the celebrity gossip.
With Eva Simpson and Caroline Hedley,
two of the *Mirror*'s 3am girls.

After losing his editorship of
the *Mirror*, Piers picked
himself up and threw himself
into writing his memoirs.

rest of Fleet Street had sat back and watched him set the agenda that they had to follow when he was editor of the *News Of The World* and now it was payback time. He had been handed the story of the century on a plate, but had a sudden and uncharacteristic attack of nerves. Many headlines surfaced about mirrors cracking. Was Fleet Street's *wunderkind* finished at thirty-one?

The answer was to be a resounding 'no', but it was touch and go for a while. In the meantime, there were ongoing concerns about the *Mirror*'s falling circulation (although this was not laid at Piers' door – it was a problem that had been going on for years), with the result that, at the beginning of 1997, a £16 million relaunch was announced. The paper was to try to make itself more female-oriented, would henceforth be known as the *Mirror*, as opposed to the *Daily Mirror*, and would take on the mighty *Sun* to boot.

Meanwhile, the *Sun* benefited enormously from a vicious price-cutting war that had seen Rupert Murdoch slash the price to gain sales and, as a consequence, the *Mirror* was falling behind. The women's pages were to be extended, Dr Miriam Stoppard hired as an agony aunt and a new showbiz column introduced. However, Piers was put on the defensive again and this time for problems not of his making.

The veteran journalist John Pilger, himself an ex-*Mirror* hand (and, it must be said, one of the most famous campaigning voices of his generation), was making a documentary on the *Mirror*'s fortunes: decline was uppermost in everyone's mind. Piers fought back and was given space in the *Guardian* to mount a defence. 'There can't be many ex-employees of the *Mirror* left alive who haven't kindly taken the trouble to air their views on how appalling the paper is recently,' he wrote. 'The *Guardian*'s own self-appointed media expert Roy Greenslade has made a career out of it. It's certainly been a more successful one than his career as an editor when he presided over one of the most spectacular drops in the *Mirror*'s circulation.'

Piers was very stung by Pilger's attack, however, and rightly pointed out that things had to change. Newspaper readership as a whole was in decline, on top of which, along with a fair number of other titles, the *Mirror* had a 'dying readership' – it was losing readers because they were literally dying off. He had to make some attempt to attract a younger audience or there would soon be no one left.

'John Pilger will have his pound of flesh this week,' he continued. 'If we get it wrong, then I will receive the traditional Fleet Street invitation to depart from my office on the twenty-second floor at Canary Wharf, head first. One thing's for sure, you won't get me turning on the *Mirror* when I leave. I have too much respect for the journalists who give their hearts and souls to making this paper a success to round on them in such a sad, sour way.'

And he was as good as his word. But the *Mirror* did have an ace up its sleeve, albeit one that owed more to circumstance than anything else: in 1997, an election was called. Since 1979, the Tories had been in power and even their biggest supporters were now acknowledging that it was time for change. The Major Government had been hanging on by the skin of its teeth (helped, some would say, by Piers' decision not to publish details of the Budget), but a massive change was in the air and the *Mirror* was a Labour-supporting paper. Time to take centre stage again.

In actual fact, when Labour won its historic victory in May 1997, by a bizarre coincidence, the *Mirror* and its great rival the *Sun* ran exactly the same front page. Both featured a huge picture of Cherie Blair kissing her husband Tony, the new British Prime Minister, with exactly the same headline: SEALED WITH A X. So similar were the front pages that the two editors were accused of acting in collusion or at least that there was a leak in one camp. Both hotly denied any such thing and poured bile on the other. 'The *Sun* dropped first and obviously the *Mirror* waited to see what our inspirational headline would be and copied it,' declared Stuart Higgins, 'but it was the *Sun* wot got it.'

Naturally, Piers did not take this lying down. 'They have had the most disastrous election in newspaper history and have finally come up with a good idea, which we had earlier in the day,' he snorted.

Certainly, the *Mirror* seemed to be doing well. The *Sun* saw a sharp drop in sales during the April leading up to the election, while the *Mirror* witnessed a rise. Piers himself put this down to the *Sun*'s sudden decision to change tack and back New Labour just six weeks before the election and he may well have been right. The *Mirror* had once sold more copies than the *Sun*, and now there were real hopes that the paper might return to the glory days of old.

Along with Stuart Higgins, Piers was summoned to Number 10 to do an interview with the new Prime Minister and, for the first time, he too was beginning to be recognised as something of a celebrity in his own right. He was certainly the pundit that everyone talked to when they wanted a quote about Fleet Street, but there was more to it than that: he was starting to stand out from the crowd in a way that he hadn't done before. Piers had certainly long been recognised among his peers for what he had achieved, but now he was reaching a wider audience – although a new career as a media personality was still some way off.

Certainly, he was completely in command of his paper now. In the summer of 1997, the country became obsessed with the relationship between Princess Diana and Dodi Fayed and there was intense competition to get the first picture of the couple kissing. The *Mirror* appeared to have done so, although, on closer inspection, it looked as if it had taken an image run by the *Mirror*'s sister paper the *People* of the couple gazing at each other on a boat and had digitally moved their positions so they seemed much closer together. It seemed the other sister paper, the *Sunday Mirror*, had acquired genuine snaps and was refusing to share them. There were rumours of shouting matches between Piers and *Sunday Mirror* editor Bridget Rowe, not least because Piers used his pictures the day before hers were due to run. The readers didn't care, though; they just wanted as much of Diana as the media could provide.

The rest of Fleet Street were more concerned, however, as Piers appeared to have stolen a march on them. There were accusations of picture manipulation and another row broke out, but Piers fought back in trademark style. Everyone did it, he claimed, pointing out there had been no complaints from readers – and, of course, this proved the case. Most hadn't even been aware of what had been done and, while the two appeared to be much closer together, there was no actual kiss as such.

If restrictions were brought in, warned Piers, 'every picture editor I know is going to have to look deep into their soul and ask themselves have they ever cropped a picture closer? Have they ever removed people from a background? Everyone does it. It doesn't change the news value or integrity of a picture. If we had had Dodi Fayed kissing Diana when they hadn't been kissing, that would have changed the integrity of that picture. We haven't had a single complaint from any reader. Why would they feel conned? I totally deny we changed the image integrity in that picture. It was quite clear, twenty-four hours later, that those two heads had been considerably closer than our picture.'

Alas, only two weeks later, HRH Princess Diana was dead. After she was killed in a car crash in Paris with Dodi on 31 August 1997, Piers suddenly discovered that he was in the midst of the biggest story in years and the papers went into overdrive, reporting on each sensational development of the case and at times actually bringing the royal family to book.

In the immediate pandemonium surrounding Diana's death, it quickly became apparent that everyone – the royal family, the political establishment and the media – was in a totally new world, making it up as they went along. As far as the media was concerned, the brutal reality was that such a huge story involving such a popular figure sold newspapers. Every newspaper competed with its peers to bring out daily supplements about the late Princess's life and a whole industry grew up not just in the days following the shocking news but for years afterwards.

But the media also reflected what the public themselves wanted to say. Most of the royal family had been at Balmoral, their castle in Scotland, when the news broke, and that, perhaps unwisely, is where they stayed. As Diana's body lay in London and preparations for the funeral began, mourners began to gather in the streets, many sobbing quite openly. New Prime Minister Tony Blair perfectly summed up the situation in a speech in which he referred to Diana as 'The People's Princess'. The nation's mood was such that it required a connection between Monarch and people, but, in a rare moment in her long reign, Queen Elizabeth II actually got it wrong.

As the royal family sheltered in Balmoral, the mood in the capital turned ugly. There had been no public message from the royals and, much in contrast to what the people wanted, there was no flag at half-mast over Buckingham Palace. The reason for this was protocol: no flag ever flew over Buckingham Palace, only the Monarch's standard, and if the Queen herself had died it wouldn't have been done. However, the people required a symbolic gesture – and no one had ever proved to be better at this than Diana herself – but the royal family simply didn't seem to understand that, at times, it is best to ignore protocol and give the people what they want.

The media is often accused of manipulating events to its own advantage; the reality is that the best papers reflect what the rest of the country feels and wants. This was an absolute case in point. As the royals appeared indifferent to the fate of the woman who had at times brought them to the brink of disaster, anger grew. And the papers, rather than whipping up indignation, merely reflected what the rest of the country thought. The headlines started to appear and the *Mirror* pictured two grieving subjects: YOUR PEOPLE ARE SUFFERING. SPEAK TO US, MA'AM ran the headline. Inside, the editorial went on, 'Now at this time, more than ever, the Queen must show she has learnt from Diana. That she understands how we are feeling.' Many of the other papers came out in similar vein.

This was new territory: while most royals had to put up with a certain degree of criticism at some point in their lives (indeed, some had to suffer a great deal), the Queen herself had been untouchable. Such was the respect and affection in which she was held that, under normal circumstances, none would have dared to criticise the Monarch. Circumstances were anything but normal now. And, to cap all that, the media suddenly found itself in the dock: Diana had been killed in a car crash as she was being chased by the paparazzi and, as her brother Earl Spencer (who had, by this time, developed a loathing for the newspapers) put it, many now believed that some sections of the media had 'blood on their hands'.

No one seemed to know what to do. In an editorial, the *Mirror* admitted it had not 'always been innocent'. Meanwhile, the *Sun* begged its readers not to cast blame. It was an extraordinary situation to be in: on the one hand, the papers were benefiting from Diana's death because people were buying them for the daily supplements and to keep up with the story; on the other, they themselves were being blamed for having had a hand in the Princess's demise.

It was announced that Diana's funeral would be held at Westminster Abbey. Most of the editors, including Piers, were invited to attend – only to be uninvited shortly afterwards by the vengeful Lord Spencer. They accepted the ruling and without attempting much of a fight back (on that point, at least) decided to stay away. Bowing to pressure, the Queen finally made a public broadcast and the family came down from Balmoral to London; they went out to inspect the numerous floral tributes left by a devoted public. Public anger towards the royals was beginning to lessen, although fury about the role of the press lingered.

When Lord Spencer spoke at his sister's funeral at Westminster Abbey, fuel was added to the flames. It was a huge affair and Spencer used the occasion to lay the blame at every door he could think of, including the royal family and the press. The Windsors were castigated for removing her HRH – she 'needed no royal title' to generate her magic, he said – before turning his attention to the press. 'She talked endlessly of getting away from England, mainly because of the treatment she received at the hands of the newspapers,' he spat. Wisely, the newspapers themselves held their counsel, although ultimately the funeral oration was seen by some as a mark of bad judgement on Spencer's part. What should have been a time of healing instead seemed to turn into an all-out war.

Piers – and the others – kept quiet on the matter but, perhaps understandably, it wasn't long before they had finally had enough. Princess Diana certainly had her fair share of media attention but, as everyone involved in the press knew at the time, she had also been an active participant. Both she and Charles had used the media in the 'War of the Waleses' and, overall, the press had been pretty much on her side. Many editors were hesitant about saying so, however, until Piers finally had his say in the *Guardian*. He cited hypocrisy, and understandably so.

'First up, with almost laughable predictability, was David Mellor, who arrived on my TV screen with indecent haste, breathlessly blaming the British tabloid press directly for the accident,' he wrote. 'Never mind the fact that we had just lost perhaps the greatest icon of our lifetime – it was far more important to have a crack at the "gutter press" than actually wait for any true details to emerge. The fact that no representation of any British tabloid was anywhere near the place at the time didn't stem his indignant rage. It was cringe-making stuff from a man with a very obvious reason for disliking newspapers that quite correctly exposed his serial adultery for the hypocrisy it was.'

Piers had put his finger on it: Earl Spencer, David Mellor and the rest all had their own issues with the press, and so, given this marvellous opportunity to blame the tabloids, they lost no time in doing so. Other sections of the press came in for equal lambasting on the grounds that they were trying to have their cake and eat it – reporting everything in salacious detail, yet criticising other papers. It was perfectly fair comment, although the saga was to run further still.

And, indeed, Earl Spencer might have reflected on the wisdom of his posturing just two months later when, back in Cape Town (where he was then resident), he went through his first divorce. The man who had attacked just about everyone for their treatment of his sister, with her eating disorders and general unhappiness, was revealed to have been an appalling husband. Victoria Lockwood, his first wife, not only had to endure repeated infidelity on his part, but was summoned to the Earl lying in his bath, whereupon he told her that he wanted a divorce and, for good measure, added that she should stay away from Diana's funeral, too.

It also emerged that Spencer first made and then withdrew an offer to shelter his sister in a property on the Althorp Estate. This was a very different picture indeed of the man who had denounced the royal family with righteous fury for its cruelty and the press had no hesitation in reporting every detail of the story.

Countess Spencer had wanted divorce proceedings to take place in London, but, no doubt thinking he would have to pay out a lower settlement, Lord Spencer insisted on Cape Town. He was probably right, in that he didn't have to pay quite as much, but had the case been heard in London then the couple's intimate details would not have been made public. His reputation never really recovered, while his sister Diana is now viewed as one of the great icons of the twentieth century.

It was poetic justice, albeit of a tragic kind.

CHAPTER SIX

KEEP OFF
THE GRASS

As the year drew to an end and the shock over the death of Diana began to fade, Piers turned his attention to other stories. The brief was as it had always been: keep the *Mirror* in the spotlight, keep the circulation moving upwards and take on the *Sun*. Any editor is only as good as the last issue and Piers knew that, to keep ahead, he would constantly have to come up with good stories to keep the *Mirror* in the limelight – which is just what he did.

In truth, his next agenda-setting triumph pretty much dropped into his lap. In December 1997, an anonymous caller rang the *Mirror* and gave it a very strong lead. 'Watch this pub, watch this bloke,' the caller advised. 'Not only will you be amazed at what he's doing, but you will also be surprised at who his parents are.'

Piers had always been aware of the advantages of sending attractive young women out on a story – indeed, he was to capitalise on this in the future with his '3am girls' – and so he duly dispatched Dawn Alford and Tanith Carey to investigate. They called in at the pub, spotted their target and shortly afterwards were deep in conversation with him, the subject moving swiftly to celebrities taking drugs. And so the target swallowed their bait, hook, line and sinker: would the girls like some drugs? On receiving an affirmative, he supplied them with what was later identified in a laboratory as £10 worth of hash.

Today, more than a decade later, there is no problem in identifying the man in question and the reason why the transaction, identical to many taking place in thousands of pubs across the country, proved such big news was that the boy in question was Will Straw, son of the then Home Secretary Jack Straw. But he was seventeen at the time, technically a juvenile, and so could not be immediately identified and was merely referred to as 'the son of a prominent Cabinet minister'. Given the sensitivities of the case, the *Mirror* had to be careful what it did next. Piers informed Straw that they had to talk about a 'private matter'. He further advised him that, if he 'came clean' and 'went public', the story would soon die down. Straw then alerted Downing Street and subsequently marched the hapless Will down to the police station, having alerted the police in advance, whereupon his son made a statement. It was agreed that everyone was acting in the correct manner – everyone except Will, who had landed himself in something of a mess.

If ever there was a good illustration of the way in which politicians (or anyone in the public eye) interrelate, this was it. Once Straw learned that the *Mirror* had the story, he won two days' reprieve before it was published, in return for which he gave the paper the information that Will had confessed to the police. The story was duly published on Christmas Eve and caused a sensation; almost immediately Will's identity became common knowledge in Fleet Street and was published in papers abroad, but he could not be identified in the UK. Meanwhile, his father – who was widely respected for his handling of the situation – made it plain to the papers that he would actually like his son to be identified in order to put an end to the speculation, but even he could do nothing for now.

In a situation where a paper can run a story, but not the identity of the person at the centre, it will do as much as it can to allow the readers to know what is really going on. And so it was that Jack Straw was time and again pictured with the pieces, ostensibly because he was the British Home Secretary and, as such, had views on drugs (his opinion was that they should not be legalised) – and actually, of course, to hint that he was the cabinet minister in question. Fuel was added to the flames when Dawn Alford was arrested for buying drugs, leading to widespread condemnation and fears that 'pressure from high places' was behind the move. Never one to flinch from battle, Piers ran the headline IS IT FAIR, MR STRAW?

Still, the reality could not be reported but the paper

was going as far as it could: OUR REPORTER IS ARRESTED IN MINISTER'S SON'S DRUG INQUIRY, it boomed in a front page featuring pictures of both Dawn Alford and Jack Straw. Certainly, this was a worrying development; it was thought no journalist had been arrested in such circumstances before. Alford had gone to the police to make a statement and pass on information; to be apprehended went against the grain but by this time the full extent of New Labour's control-freak tendencies was becoming apparent. The party was developing a reputation for coming down hard on anyone who dared to cross it, and for a journalist and newspaper to expose a senior New Labour figure's son was clearly beyond the pale. There was an unpleasant smack of authoritarianism about it, especially given that everyone concerned had bent over backwards to behave in the correct manner.

But, if this was an attempt to dampen the story down, it didn't work. And it wasn't just the *Mirror* who reacted with fury; correctly sensing an attack on a free press, so too did everyone else. 'Is Britain's elite suppressing the truth once again?' asked one paper. 'Shameful bid to gag press,' roared another. Indeed, the story, which had by now dominated the papers for over a week and once seemed in danger of fizzling out altogether, went straight back on to all the front pages, with Piers adopting a 'more-in sadness-than-in-anger' position.

'I can't imagine in a million years they will charge her,' he said, 'it would be totally ridiculous. But I didn't imagine in a million years they would arrest her. I don't think Labour have handled it very well. My advice from the start was that, if they came clean, it would go away. I think now, perhaps with hindsight, they wish they had.' The matter had now become such an open secret as to who was at the centre of the story that soon there would be no further need for discretion, he believed. 'Within a week, everybody will know who this cabinet minister is,' he continued. 'It does seem rather absurd to carry on the pretence that it can remain secret.'

In the event, the *Mirror* would not be the first to name the family at the centre of the case. In early January 1998, it was obvious that the farce couldn't go on. One of the problems was that the *Sun* had been on the verge of naming the family but had been prevented from doing so after the Attorney General John Morris took out an injunction. This was now overturned – behind the scenes, Jack Straw himself had been briefing journalists that he would like to come out in the open – and, finally, the family was named. Will Straw's identity was such common knowledge that it was said London taxi drivers had been letting their passengers in on the secret. Now, at last, it was no longer a secret.

It was clearly a relief for Jack Straw to be able to talk openly about it: he'd found the situation as ludicrous as everyone else. 'I felt the same emotions as any parents would in such circumstances – those of shock and concern,' he said, in a prepared statement. 'Being a parent means giving love and support, and, when it's necessary, confronting children with their wrongdoing. When a child does wrong, I believe it to be the duty of a parent to act promptly. That is what I sought to do. My son went voluntarily with me to the police. He did not, and should not, expect any favours from the legal process. He will accept and suffer any sanctions that arise, though, like any parents, we stand by him. But I hope that everyone who reports this story will agree that he should not suffer additionally from being my son.'

In the event, Straw junior received a caution and the matter was then closed – except that it wasn't entirely. There was some sanctimonious comment from certain quarters as to how the story should never have been run at all and this despite the fact that it was the son of the Home Secretary: very nearly an adult and a boy who had put his parents in a terrible position.

And while all the charges against Dawn Alford were dropped, she was still livid about the comment from various quarters that it was one step away from entrapment and she had been put on the story because she was a pretty girl. 'Despite the enormous contribution women make to newspapers, we are still being dismissed as mere dollies with Dictaphones,' she snapped.

Piers, too was irritated. 'Dawn Alford has been the subject of some pretty unseemly smears in other sections of the media because of the way she looks,' he said. 'People have forgotten she has been doing this for five years. She's not just somebody we picked for the newsroom because we thought she'd look good to send down to ensnare William Straw. She is a very experienced investigative journalist.

'I think it's very sexist and insulting that she's had to be singled out just because of the way she looks. I think there is a lot of jealousy and envy in certain areas. My experience of these things is eventually the story dies a natural death and that's the time the press get a kicking. At the end of the day, where would the broadsheets have been without this story for the last three weeks?'

Whatever the truth behind the sniping, Piers had once more set the news agenda. It was an opportune moment for his old friend and mentor Kelvin MacKenzie to step forward again; he was appointed deputy chief executive and group managing director at the Mirror Group, thus effectively taking charge of three newspapers: the *Mirror*, *Sunday Mirror* and the *People*. Piers' critics (and there were a lot of them) cited this as proof that he wasn't up to the job and MacKenzie had been brought in over his head, but the truth was different: Piers had proved himself over and over, while his mentor had been away from the industry he knew best and in which he was most successful: newspapers. This was just a way of harnessing his expertise in a very difficult market. Kelvin himself had been partially responsible for Piers' appointment and was hardly going to step in to sabotage his protégé.

And Piers was having no difficulties with setting the agenda on his own. In early 1998, Mohamed al-Fayed (father of Dodi al-Fayed, Princess Diana's lover who was killed with her in the Paris car crash) voiced his suspicions in the pages of the *Mirror* that the two had been murdered. As it transpired, those suspicions would continue to make the front pages of newspapers for many years to come.

Indeed, Princess Diana was proving to be just as fascinating in death as she had been in life. There had been only one survivor of the Paris car crash – Dodi's bodyguard, Trevor Rees-Jones – and he gave his first ever interview to the *Mirror*, boosting sales by 400,000, or 20 per cent. He said that he vaguely remembered a woman crying out – 'I have had flashes of a female voice calling out in the back of the car, then Dodi's name is called. It can only have been Princess Diana.' He also said there was no sign that the driver of the car, Henri Paul, was drunk. The interview was carried out by Piers himself and took place at Harrods, then owned by Mohamed al-Fayed, amid widespread suspicions that al-Fayed was pulling strings behind the interview, although this was hotly denied by everyone involved.

Rees-Jones was upset enough by the reaction to issue a statement in which he made it clear that he had not been paid for the interview and had gone public entirely independently of al-Fayed simply because of the huge public interest in the case. But this was not to be the end of the matter; some years later, he wrote a book about his experiences and, a full decade after the interview, he was to appear at Diana's inquest. One of the problems was that the crash had been so traumatic that it had impaired his memory: he was the only survivor and yet he had no recollection of what really happened, although in later years he was to put it on record that he thought the crash had been an accident and nothing more.

Piers was expert at knowing what would sell newspapers, but so, too, it turned out, was the Prime Minister, Tony Blair. A very canny operator when it came to the media, Blair had launched a full-on charm offensive when first elected Leader of the Labour Party in 1994 and was continuing with it now that he was in office. The *Mirror* was a Labour-supporting paper anyway, and so he could be pretty sure of backing, but he was taking no chances. Piers was fast becoming a regular visitor to 10 Downing Street (although, as he later admitted, there was no love lost between himself and Cherie) and also on occasion interviewed the PM.

As the controversy continued over Diana's death, Blair gave an emotional interview about how he still missed her personally. 'Diana had an enormous amount to contribute to this country and, indeed, she was contributing an enormous amount to this country,' he said. 'I am convinced she would have contributed an awful lot more if it had not been for the accident. It was, and remains, a tragedy for everyone.'

Piers observed then that Blair's 'hold on the populist pulse is truly remarkable' and he was right: at the time, the new Prime Minister was an enormously popular figure, with the chaos of his later years still almost inconceivable. He was widely credited for having all but saved the Monarchy from itself when it appeared not to understand the depth of public feeling in the wake of Diana's death but was careful to play this down. 'We had to keep our focus on the royal family itself, which was going through enormous difficulty and grief at the time,' he said. 'We had to make sure they were properly supported. We had to keep our nerve. In a situation like that there are no rules and no training. You do what you think is right by instinct. I was very proud of the work my team did, but I want to stress very strongly that the royal family, and in particular the Queen, was very sensitive to how people felt.'

In those far-off days, Blair's instinct was faultless: he knew exactly how to connect to the British people – as did Piers. Of course, it's impossible to compare a newspaper editor and a prime minister (although editors have a good deal more power than all but the most senior politicians), but Piers' own instinct for what made the British tick was unerring – it was rare for him to misjudge the public mood, although, like Blair, he was to do so when it came to the War in Iraq. But he could just tell what the readers and the wider public wanted and this was one of the reasons why he was to do so well in later years as an interviewer and a judge on reality TV.

This became apparent in one small gesture. In March 1998, a silver cup came to auction from a school – West

Heath – that had closed down the previous year. It was awarded to pupils who excelled at tap and ballet. Entirely unremarkable except for one small feature, it would normally have been worth no more than £15 to £20. But that small feature was a line which read: 'D Spencer 1976'. It was the cup that had been presented to Princess Diana when she was still at school and dreamed of becoming a ballerina. As such, it was worth far more than that. And so, when it went up for auction, none other than the *Mirror* itself bought it and turned the purchase into a publicity coup when it was announced that they would be giving it to Princes William and Harry, as well as having a replica of the cup made to be presented each year to a child with exceptional dancing skills.

'We felt it was right that this trophy should be passed to her two sons rather than to a stranger at an auction house, given the obvious sentimental value,' said Piers, completely in tune with the prevailing sentiment at the time.

And he had showed that he could learn from his mistakes, too. In the wake of the ACHTUNG! SURRENDER front page and because of the forthcoming international event taking place once more, the Press Complaints Commission chairman Lord Wakeham warned the papers not to incite 'violence, disorder or xenophobia' during their coverage of the World Cup. A penitent Piers held up his hands. 'The bottom line was that readers didn't like it very much,' he said. 'What Euro '96 showed was that that kind of humour, which had been pretty well acceptable in the tabloids for quite a few years before, had really reached its end. People were saying enough was enough. When we went too far with the Germany game, we all sat down and thought, "Right, we mustn't let that happen again." We took that old-style humour too far. You can still be humorous, but you shouldn't be offensive. The readers won't put up with it. Our coverage will be very different.'

Lessons, as they say, had been learned; Piers could afford to be somewhat regretful, given that he'd been setting the agenda day in and day out with other royal stories, as well as enjoying cosy chats with the PM, but he was now signalling to the world in general – and his industry in particular – that here was a wiser, more mature version of himself. Utterly in tune with *Mirror* readers, he knew exactly what was expected of him and, in the years to come, he wasn't about to disappoint. Finally, the Boy Wonder had grown up.

CHAPTER SEVEN

A CONTROVERSIAL SIDE

As Piers settled into the job, there were increasing signs that the *Mirror* was going to be an independent voice when it came to the Labour Party. Overall, it would be supportive but it would not be slow to criticise, as and when occasion demanded. This stance was hardened during a row involving the then US President Bill Clinton when Piers thought it would be a good idea to run an open letter from Clinton to the people of Ulster in the run-up to the referendum. Clinton agreed, so long as the *Mirror* penned the actual copy. The paper's political editor, Kevin Maguire, duly obliged, but when a copy was sent for approval to Tony Blair's director of communications, Alastair Campbell, he also sent a copy to the *Sun*, who then put it on the front page. Piers went ballistic and the ensuing row was virulent enough for the rest of Fleet Street to admit there was no question that he really was his own man now.

Over at the *Sun*, the paper's editor Stuart Higgins suddenly and unexpectedly resigned, to be replaced by David Yelland, which signalled the onset of a fresh feud. Piers said that he would give him 'the mother of all welcomes, just to make him feel at home', and, indeed, no love was lost between the two men over the next few years.

In fact, theirs was to be a personal animosity, far more than is usually found between the editors of two rival newspapers. Piers could be savage when he wanted to be. 'They [the *Sun*] appear to be slightly more puerile than normal without the sharp cutting edge of humour that Kelvin always brought to the party,' he declared. 'They seem a bit stupid. Mr Yelland is a bright guy, wholly unsuited to his job – he will prove a glorious failure and I wish him every success.'

Naturally, Yelland replied in kind, although in truth his appointment had caused astonishment in some quarters. He would never have quite the populist touch of his rival and didn't seem to understand the way in which attitudes in Britain were changing. His paper notoriously asked, IS BRITAIN BEING RUN BY A GAY MAFIA? after the former Welsh secretary Ron Davies was discovered in dubious circumstances on Clapham Common, but, rather than chiming with the readers as it would have done a decade earlier, the piece instead provoked accusations of homophobia.

Meanwhile, Piers was managing to take a more liberal line, while thoroughly enjoying himself at the expense of the *Sun*; in the wake of the homophobia accusations, the paper piously declared that it would only out people if it was in the public interest to do so. Piers promptly published an article with the title SETTING SUN: 'The *Sun* has done so many U-turns in the past few days, it must be in danger of vanishing up its own dwindling circulation,' he jeered.

Not that his own style of editing was without controversy: at the time, Piers was getting his knuckles rapped for running a series of articles about Prince Harry. They were actually pretty minor stories, all about new haircuts and slight sports injuries, but, in the wake of the death of Princess Diana, the media had to tread carefully where other royals, especially her sons, were concerned. But he wasn't going to be pushed around; on learning that Prince Charles was considering making a complaint to the Press Complaints Commission regarding a story about Harry hurting his arm, Piers threatened to launch an investigation of his own into stories leaked by those surrounding the royals themselves to cast them in a more flattering light.

'It will be a comprehensive review into the number of stories that have emanated from St James's Palace in the last year, which place them in a favourable light,' he declared. 'We think the public have a right to know.' This was a robust reaction, but a high-risk strategy, too – in the wake of Diana's death, it was easy for feelings to run high.

By now, Piers had really grown into the job of editor

and relished the attention it brought. In hindsight, there are clear signs about the direction his life was about to follow, too. 'Sure, occasionally I get called a complete tosser but it doesn't bother me,' he insisted in an interview at the time. 'If you are my age [thirty-three] and you do my job, you are going to get attention. And I don't exactly run from that – it gets attention for the paper. If the BBC and ITV want to come and interview me, it saves thousands of pounds in advertising. If you are not the market leader, you have to try every trick in the book to get attention for your paper and that has very much been my strategy.'

He simply never stopped. Hot on the heels of rowing with the royals, he became involved in a massive feud with *Guardian* editor Alan Rusbridger, whom he accused of stealing a *Mirror* story; it was a big one, the fact that Peter Mandelson, then the Secretary of State for Trade and Industry, had borrowed a large sum from Geoffrey Robinson, then the Paymaster General, to buy his Notting Hill home. Rusbridger denied point-blank that he had stolen the story. The problem was that another columnist who Piers had recently hired, Paul Routledge, had recently written a biography of Mandelson and included the story about the loan. However, the *Mirror* didn't publish the piece but then it seems someone at the *Guardian* saw the manuscript, picked up on the story and claimed it for their own, whereupon another row ensued, before the two were spotted having dinner at The Ivy.

Piers also claimed that Prince Michael of Kent was in

debt to the tune of £2.5 million, another story roundly condemned as lies. The paper also serialised *Monica's Story*, Andrew Morton's biography of Bill Clinton's intern and near-nemesis Monica Lewinsky.

Scoop after scoop followed, with huge dollops of self-publicity thrown in, and it was announced that Piers was to edit, as a one-off, an issue of the women's magazine *Cosmopolitan*.

Financially, Piers was doing well, too. Home was now a large house in Wandsworth, South London, and a tailor regularly visited him at his office. Holidays were spent in the Caribbean and he frequented the finest restaurants while his two sons, Spencer and Stanley, attended private school. As well as eating in the best restaurants, he was also beginning to appear at the best parties. Slowly, but surely, Piers was becoming a celebrity in his own right.

And still the scoops rolled in. The latest was the publication of love letters written thirty years previously by Moors murderer Ian Brady to Myra Hindley; Brady threatened to go to court to get them back.

Piers may have sort of made up with Alan Rusbridger, but he was more than prepared to re-feud when it suited his own ends. When Rusbridger and his deputy Georgina Henry held an online chat on the *Guardian* website (still something of a novelty back then), Piers logged on as Piers 10 and posted the following message: 'Congratulations on making The Guardian even more unreadable than it was before'.

Rusbridger and Henry refused to let this pass. 'Piers 10,' they posted. 'Why don't you stick to narcissistic (look it up) phone-in polls and leave the real journalism to journalists?'

But they were also pretty good sports. Piers' contribution had been so lively (he went on to say that, if he printed a picture of Rusbridger's behind, he would still get more readers in East Darlington than the *Guardian* achieved nationally) that the readers loved it – and so he was invited back on to the *Guardian* website to become the subject of a chat himself.

Piers' continued interest in the royal family – or, to be more specific, his numerous stories about them, especially one focusing on an injury Prince Harry received when playing rugby – actually prompted a ruling by the Press Complaints Committee, which published a new set of guidelines as to how the papers must behave. The boys should not be constantly under the spotlight, it stated, but at the same time St James's Palace would have to accept there was an enormous amount of interest in them. As well he might, Piers welcomed the ruling.

In May 1999 came another masterstroke: this time with the establishment of the first Pride of Britain Awards, something that was to become an annual feature at the *Mirror* and continues to this day. The idea was simple: give awards to ordinary people who have done outstanding things, and invite the great and good along. Inspirational teachers were honoured, along with bomb victims and courageous children. The A-list was out in force, including Tony and Cherie Blair, Mo Mowlam, Queen Noor of Jordan, various Spice Girls (then at the height of their fame), as well as Sir Paul McCartney and Heather Mills. In fact, this was where the couple first met, something Piers was to dine out on for many years ahead. It was a spectacular success.

Over at the *Sun*, David Yelland looked as if he was proving the doubters right. Usually, Piers was the one accused of going too far, but this time it was unquestionably his rival; in the run-up to the wedding of Prince Edward and Sophie Rhys-Jones, the *Sun* published a picture taken years earlier of Sophie with her right breast exposed. The uproar was immediate, so much so that the *Sun* was forced to apologise almost straight away. For Piers, who was so often the person who had pushed the envelope, the moment must have been sweet: this knocked stories about Prince Harry into a cocked hat. And not in a good way, as far as the *Sun* was concerned. Piers was also not slow to gloat: he put the story on the front page, two inside pages and a comment slot, as David Yelland was forced to issue one grovelling apology after another. In truth, Piers himself had been there many a time , even so, it was nice to see the boot on the other foot. There were even reports that Piers would be headhunted to return to News International and edit the *Sun*, although these rumours proved wide of the mark.

Still, he triumphed at the *Mirror*, where the paper

had taken it upon itself to campaign for a memorial for Princess Diana. In September 1999, the building of just such a tribute was announced. But he was still able to laugh at himself, for, when the *Mirror* published a Power 100 List, Piers was at number 78. (David Yelland also appeared, under the name David Tharg and was described as the 'current' editor of the *Sun*.)

Piers had certainly proved his doubters wrong: he entered his fourth year as editor of the *Mirror* more than ever his own man. Both Kelvin MacKenzie and David Montgomery had now left, which meant he was no longer plagued by stories about the two of them breathing down his neck, while he had taken the paper slightly upmarket and given it a more feel-good stance than the *Sun*.

At that stage, his marriage was still quite happy; his sons were turning out to be almost as football mad as himself and life seemed good. Yet another scoop landed on his desk: Cherie Blair was pregnant. The *Mirror* triumphed yet again!

It was to continue to do so, but Piers very nearly found himself in serious trouble yet again. More than once in his career, it happened that, just as matters were going extremely well, he almost managed to sabotage himself and so it was to prove again. But this time around, it wasn't an ill-judged front page or yet another feud but something far worse: there were suggestions of financial impropriety and Piers was to find himself at the centre of the story, an experience he only just survived.

The trouble began in the *Mirror*'s 'City' pages. At that stage, two extremely aggressive young men, Anil Bhoyrul and James Hipwell, operated under the name 'City Slickers', the title under which the scandal was to become known. They tipped a company called Viglen, a computer hardware company belonging to Sir Alan Sugar under the title, SUGAR TO JOIN NET GOLD RUSH, and the shares subsequently soared. However, it then emerged that, the night before the story appeared, Piers had bought £20,000 worth of Viglen Technology through Kyte Securities, a stake holding which promptly doubled when the price soared from 181p to 366p. It didn't look good, although it should be noted that he bought the shares in his own name and, had he been up to no good, this would not have been the brightest of ideas.

But, as soon as the facts came to light, there was outrage. Shares do soar on the back of newspaper tips, which means stringent regulations have been set as to what journalists are permitted to buy. Meanwhile, Piers was adamant he'd done nothing wrong. 'It [the share purchase] was nothing to do with the column,' he insisted. 'I never see the "City" column before the market shuts. The first I see of it is around 6.30pm or 7pm. I was amused when I saw it. I was going to buy them anyway; I believe in Alan Sugar, he is a columnist here and it is a good company. Everyone was tipping them. I don't buy that many shares and I am scrupulous about how I do it. I would never do anything improper – I don't go sneaking over to see what the tip of the day is.'

Nonetheless, he had ruffled a few feathers over previous years and his detractors were not slow to leap on this one. Whatever the truth – and Piers was later completely exonerated – it did not look good. The Stock Exchange announced it would be launching an investigation while the *Mirror*'s management summoned their editor to explain himself. He was forced to issue a public statement. 'I did not personally feel the article was particularly market-sensitive,' he said. 'I was therefore very surprised when the share price doubled the next morning but I made no attempt to sell any shares then and I have not done so since. I have not breached the Code of Conduct or any Stock Exchange regulations. My purchase of the shares was made six hours before the City Slickers obtained their story from Viglen's chief executive and, if I was going to buy shares in a company based on information from the paper, would I be stupid enough to do it in my own name?'

It goes without saying that the *Sun* was beside itself with glee at the story, and it's a measure of just how seriously it was taken that the matter was raised in the House of Commons. There were widespread calls for Piers to be sacked, while attention was turned to the 'City Slickers' themselves (who were to pay a much higher price). Like so many of his journalists, they had been encouraged to turn themselves into personalities and thus had also made a few enemies along the way, so more than one rival would be glad to see them come down.

Meanwhile, Piers appeared to have suddenly become

aware of just how much trouble he was in. While continuing to deny any wrongdoing, *Mirror* insiders said that an air of embarrassment hung about him, that he was uncharacteristically glum. The story had made every other paper, from his immediate rivals to the broadsheets.

So, had Piers Morgan, Boy-Wonder-turned-tabloid-legend, finally taken a step too far?

CHAPTER EIGHT

READ ALL ABOUT IT

The fact that Piers was news was nothing unusual – ever since his 'Bizarre' days, he had been one of the most high-profile journalists in town. But this time around was different: the Department of Trade and Industry had been called in to make an investigation and he looked to be in serious trouble. What's more, there seemed to be no shortage of people wishing him ill. He had gained many admirers along the way but an awful lot of enemies, too, and there was nothing many of them would have liked more than to see him come completely unstuck.

The Press Complaints Commission's Code of Practice was quite clear about it: Clause 14 made the following points:

- Even where the law does not prohibit it, journalists must not use for their own profit financial information they receive in advance of its general publication. Nor should they pass such information to others.

- Journalists must not write about shares or securities in whose performance they know that they or their close families have a significant financial interest without disclosing the interest to the editor or financial editor.
- They must not buy or sell, either directly or through nominees or agents, shares or securities about which they have written recently or intend to write about in the near future.

Appearance was everything and it didn't look good: for a man who made his living from running stories about the weaknesses of others, even the suggestion that something dodgy had been going on in his own life was alarming. Meanwhile, none of his rivals was keen to let go: scenting blood, the pack gave chase.

The Press Complaints Commission got involved after a complaint was made and, although questions were asked at Prime Minister's Question Time in the House of Commons, Tony Blair declined to comment. Piers was forced to issue a lengthy statement in which he denied point-blank knowing his paper was tipping the shares before he did the deal. As uproar mounted, he sold his shares and pledged to give the £13,900 profit to charity. Further investigations were then announced: this time into Anil Bhoyrul, one of the 'City Slickers' himself.

And the *Sun* certainly wasn't about to hold itself back. It ran stories about sleaze at the *Mirror* and accused Piers of being like Robert Maxwell, the paper's former owner and a plunderer of the company's pension fund. James Hipwell, the other 'City Slicker', also came under investigation – both Slickers were accused of hyping shares they owned – and even Tina Weaver, the paper's deputy editor, was suspected of buying shares that had been plugged. Reporters were now beginning to surround Piers' house in South London. He himself had been only too happy to dish out this treatment to others, but it was not so much fun being on the receiving end.

As the scandal rumbled on, other firms were caught up in it, too. Bloomberg, the financial news agency, very publicly warned its staff not to deal in shares of companies they were writing about. At the same time, the *Sun* published a headline about the Slickers, which simply read: SPIVS. By now, they were devoting whole pages to 'Mirrorgate', piling on the pressure and revelling in the discomfort they could cause their adversary. Piers fought back, accusing the *Sun*'s City editor Ian King of owning shares he had tipped, and editor David Yelland threatened to sue.

Matters escalated further. Piers was threatened with even more embarrassment when it emerged that he stood to make £500,000 on another share tipped by his paper; there was no suggestion of impropriety, but he had previously bought £10,000 worth of shares in Corporate Executive Search (CES) at 5p each. Shares were subsequently suspended (this was normal practice) when the company announced that it was to buy an internet company and, when trading started up again, it was speculated the shares could rise to 250p (in the event, this didn't happen). Piers himself had done nothing wrong, but once again the *Mirror* had tipped the company. Trinity Mirror, owner of the *Mirror*, publicly backed its editor on the grounds that the paper had plugged the shares while they were still suspended and the move was therefore not price-sensitive.

The 'City Slickers' themselves were summarily dismissed, though without Piers' knowledge. As was Anthony Laiker, Piers' broker at Kyte Securities, who had made share deals for another fourteen of the staff on the newspaper. At this point, the Stock Exchange began to examine hours of tapes of Piers talking to Laiker, around whom there was now intense speculation as to why he was going. Meanwhile, Kyte stayed schtum, and the *Sun* ran a huge story about Piers facing a possible jail sentence. The 'City Slickers' declared their loyalty to their former editor. 'Piers did not know that we were being fired,' insisted Anil Bhoyrul. 'He was very angry, I do not blame him.'

But the former columnists' loyalty was not to last for Bhoyrul subsequently launched a legal action against the *Mirror* for unfair dismissal. 'We were doing nothing wrong. The company needed to find some scapegoats,' he insisted. 'I've tipped about 2,000 shares in the column: I've had shares in maybe five of those and I'm always very open about those shares.'

As the furore raged on and speculation intensified that Piers might now be forced out, Sir Victor Blank, chairman of Trinity Mirror, publicly backed his editor, insisting his position was secure. Another row then broke out when it emerged that Piers had not bought the shares in his own name but in that of a nominee – although, again, this was standard practice. The Stock Exchange widened its investigation to include a third deal, this time into shares in Wiggins Group, which Piers had bought and were subsequently tipped by his paper, which continued to back him. And, if that was not enough, it then emerged that Tina Weaver had previously nominated Anil Bhoyrul as Financial Journalist of the Year.

Piers then took a much-needed week off to go on holiday and Tina Weaver edited the paper in his absence. Meanwhile, David Yelland announced that, had he been in Piers' position, he would most certainly have stood down. The 'City Slickers', having been loyal to their erstwhile editor for about a week, let it be known that they would not be standing by him and he might have seen their share-tipping column hours earlier than he first said. Everything hinged on the timing of when Piers initially saw the copy: if it was after he had purchased the shares, then he was in the clear but, if it was before, this was a different story. Piers returned from holiday to be met by calls for his resignation from senior Labour MPs – it was looking extremely bad.

Somehow, he toughed it out, although whether it was

wise to do so was another matter. In hindsight, it is possible to say that, although it took another four years before his enemies forced him out, Piers' reputation remained tarnished even after the whole episode calmed down. In fact, he was completely cleared of any wrongdoing after exhaustive investigations by everyone from the Department of Trade and Industry to those working on his own newspaper, but mud sticks and this extremely unpleasant affair proved only a precursor to what would happen when he finally had to step down.

One noteworthy aspect, however, was that Piers' own staff really did not want him to leave. He was popular among *Mirror* employees (although less so with former hacks at the newspaper) and many were now beginning to feel that the attacks on their editor were, to a certain extent, attacks on the newspaper itself, and, although Piers' paper profit on the CES shares now turned out to be about £80,000, his staff were beginning to want the whole story to go away. There was also the feeling that some Labour MPs were truly relishing the situation – after all, the *Mirror* might still be a Labour-biased newspaper but it certainly didn't hesitate to criticise when criticism was due. With Piers gone, the *Mirror* may have toed the party line a little more but he wasn't going any time soon and so his colleagues simply had to wait for the furore to die down. Even Rupert Murdoch stuck the boot into his former editor, saying that, if he had been working for him at this point, he would have been fired.

Of course, Piers had walked out but, even so, this was a wounding comment.

Gradually, life began to return to normal. Not that controversy was ever far away: in March 2000, Trevor Rees-Jones retracted his claim to have heard Princess Diana's last words, in direct contradiction to what he had told Piers. At this point, Piers promptly ran an editorial in which he warned Rees-Jones not to try to profit from the death of Diana, although the former bodyguard went on to write a book anyway. And the shares scandal certainly simmered on the backburner for many years to come; in December 2005, 'City Slicker' James Hipwell admitted to dealing in the shares of forty companies he had recommended to readers of the *Mirror*. The story was to run and run.

With spectacularly bad timing, given the recent controversy, the *Mirror* was sued by Victor Kiam, the tycoon who liked Remington razors so much he bought the company. An article had appeared in the 'City Slickers' column in which it was claimed that Kiam was about to put Ronson – a company he had just bought – into receivership. In fact, he was doing nothing of the sort and won the libel case. With the departure of the two Slickers, the whole column had been abandoned but, given that the *Mirror* desperately wanted to forget its entire recent history, this was yet more all-round embarrassment. An increasingly irate Anil Bhoyrul gave an interview to the *Press Gazette* with his version of events, declaring, 'I won't be the fall guy.'

Amid all this pressure, Piers had somehow managed to stay relatively calm but, at the British Press Awards in March 2000, he found himself no longer able to keep his feelings under control, berating various people present for their comments about his travails. Completely tired of all the stick he had been receiving, he even cancelled a speech to the Confederation of British Industry. Certainly, he'd had his fair share of controversy in the past, but nothing like this; the ACHTUNG! SURRENDER headline might have been a mistake but not along these lines. Altogether, this was a foretaste of what it was to really fall foul of the pack – although, on the whole, odd rant aside, he managed to keep his head down.

Still, at least he had the Pride of Britain Awards, which ran for the second time in 2000 and was just as successful as the first time around. Blair was there again (sitting between Michael Caine and Diana Ross), along with a real A-list – it was a welcome respite from all the jibes Piers had recently been receiving.

In the event, the Press Complaints Commission issued a strong rebuke, advising him that he had 'fallen short of the high professional standards demanded by the Code'. If that were not enough, it added, 'In view of the unsatisfactory state of affairs revealed by this episode, the Commission has decided to refer the terms of this adjudication to the chief executive of Trinity Mirror' – in other words, they were reporting Piers to his boss. But Sir Victor Blank had already made it quite clear that he would be standing behind his editor, and so it was that Piers lived to fight another day.

In June 2000, matters took a turn for the better when it was announced that Piers and Marion were expecting their third child in six months' time. He also proved himself to have a considerably more forgiving nature – to say nothing of a sense of irony – when he hired a new City columnist, Suzy Jagger. It was Ms Jagger who had printed the original story about Piers' share-dealing activities in the *Daily Telegraph*, thus setting the whole story in motion, but it showed that Piers had not lost his instinct for good publicity because his latest signing certainly got him noticed. It even made him look like a good sport, all the more so when Piers himself nominated Suzy for an award for 'Scoop of the Year'.

And he certainly couldn't keep away from the limelight. In 1998, Piers had taken possession of some love letters written by Princess Diana to Major James Hewitt after the former Cavalry officer's then girlfriend, Anna Ferretti, attempted to sell them. While Piers did not publish the letters, nor did he return them on the grounds that they really belonged to Diana's family and, over two years later, he was now being questioned about the matter by Scotland Yard, although he was never actually charged with theft. Naturally, he responded in his usual robust way.

'I understand that James Hewitt accuses me of conspiring with others to steal from him letters written to him by the late Diana, Princess of Wales,' he said. 'I do not believe there is any evidence to support this allegation. The *Mirror* was approached by a woman called Anna Ferretti, who offered to sell to the *Mirror* for some £150,000 personal letters written to James Hewitt by Diana. Ferretti [said] she was not acting on behalf of Hewitt, but I believed she was, as she was an intimate friend and I knew he had previously exploited the letters for his personal gain. It was decided to pretend to Ferretti that the *Mirror* would buy the letters but give them to Diana's representatives and refuse payment of the £150,000. The broad facts have been well known since shortly after they occurred, not least because they were published in the *Mirror* in April 1998, and I am astonished that I should be accused of criminal activity, especially after all this time and consider it an abuse of process.'

In the event, the matter was laid to rest but that was just one of many controversies with which Piers was dealing at the time. Another, though perhaps more of an innovation, was the establishment of a new style of gossip column – the lifeblood of any tabloid newspaper – on the *Mirror*. As already noted, this had been the means whereby Piers himself had risen to fame and he now took a similar approach to his own staff: make the journalists themselves the stars of the gossip column, while at the same time making it appear as if they are an integral part of the world they are reporting on. And so he created a new column called '3am' and picked three attractive women – Polly Graham, Eva Simpson and Jessica Callan

– to front it. Their mission was to attend every showbiz event going and be photographed with the stars; all three were so successful that they built careers on the back of '3am'. The writers attracted a great deal of attention (all of which, of course, reflected well on Piers and the *Mirror*), while Piers himself talked of them as his 'James Bonds'.

All this was a welcome distraction from the furore over the 'City Slickers' column – and from Piers' private life, too, for the arrival of his third son Albert had not managed to paper over the increasingly obvious cracks in his marriage to Marion, and the relationship was nearing an end. However, a new romance was beginning, which came to light in an unusual way. Rumours went round Fleet Street like a flash when the news broke: a journalist called Marina Hyde, working on the *Sun*, had been summarily sacked with no notice – and the reason for this was that a lengthy email exchange between herself and Piers had come to light.

Of course, Marina was working on the *Sun*, whose biggest rival was the *Mirror*, which Piers edited. Worse still, she was also on the showbiz desk. Initially, it seemed there were suspicions that she could have been passing on information to her paper's rival until Piers himself intervened and said that the emails were in fact of a purely personal nature. In many ways, however, this only made matters worse: though neither was exactly forthcoming, it appeared that Piers had approached Marina with a view to poaching her to come and work at the *Mirror*, but, instead, his interest had quickly become personal. Both were married but the relationship soon turned into a full-blown affair. Once again, and for the last time, Piers left his wife, Marion.

The relationship with Marina was not to last either, but for a time it was all anyone could talk about. Roger Eastoe, the managing director of Mirror Newspapers, left in October 2000, but Piers was not present as he was making an appearance on the BBC's *Question Time* and was therefore unable to hear his old friend Kelvin MacKenzie quip, 'I'm terribly sorry Piers Morgan can't be with us, but he's elsewhere recording *Question Time* and the first question is from his mistress, and the second question is from his wife.'

At this point, Piers and Marina had not actually moved in together – he was staying with Martin Crudace, a lawyer for the Mirror Group – but his marriage was effectively over, although it was to be many years before the divorce finally came through. Nor could he complain about the treatment he was getting, considering how many stories he himself had run about other people's personal lives. There was also some amusement that, when Marina appealed against the decision to sack her, she actually brought Piers into the News International headquarters to speak on her behalf – the editor of the *Mirror* in the very heart of the lair of its enemy! She did not win her appeal, but shortly afterwards turned up as a columnist on the *Guardian*, where, at the time of writing, she still resides.

Piers didn't go public on the matter but clearly felt stung, and a leader appeared in the *Mirror*, into which much could be read. 'Email has created a whole new breed of ghastly snoopers who sneakily read private memos sent by their employees to friends or family when there is no commercial sensitivity involved,' it read. Was this a coded message to David Yelland, editor of the *Sun*? Many believed it to be just that.

At any rate, Piers was in no position to complain, given his own enthusiastic researches into other people's lives. In early 2001, there was a row when the *Mirror* ran a picture of the supermodel Naomi Campbell leaving a Narcotics Anonymous clinic. Campbell promptly sued, which led to further concerns that Piers' own actions might be setting in place a privacy law. Meanwhile, he himself professed to be unconcerned.

In 2001, the Pride of Britain Awards played host to the likes of Lord Robert Winston, Simon Weston, Sir Richard Branson, and Richard and Judy – if nothing else, Piers was proving that he could still pull in the A-list crowd. He had, for him, been remarkably quiet of late; even for a man as capable of snatching victory from the jaws of defeat as him, it had been a bruising two years. The shadow of the 'City Slickers' continued to loom large and, however much he might personally have wanted to ignore the whole affair, it simply refused to go away.

The DTI investigation continued, but Piers received a very public vote of confidence from the board of Trinity

Mirror when, in April 2001 (now aged thirty-six), he signed a contract for a further five years of editing the *Mirror* and was also made the *Sunday Mirror*'s editor-in-chief. The *Sunday Mirror*'s actual editor was now Tina Weaver, his erstwhile deputy and someone who had been named in the share-dealing scandal. Piers was publicly pleased. 'I have regularly throughout this, particularly at the start, thought that a lot of lesser managements would have turfed me straight out the door,' he said. 'I thought that from the first week onwards when it really began to accelerate and the *Sun* really stuck the boot in. And I've been absolutely staggered by the support from the company led by Victor and Philip Graf and the rest of the board, who have all stuck their necks out for me and refused to alter their position.

'We all know the DTI are continuing their investigation and no one can say with 100 per cent certainty how that will end because we're not them. I remain confident, like the company does, that I did nothing wrong. But, until that position changes, they are perfectly entitled to carry on business as usual.'

He was also adamant that the picture drawn of the *Mirror* as a place where half the staff seemed to be playing the markets was totally false. 'The culture's a great myth,' he declared. 'Hardly anybody on the floor bought shares and hardly anybody had any connection with any Slickers' tips at all. It was a countrywide culture of piling into new technology stocks. Clearly, when you go back now and study the language [the Slickers] used, it looks like everything's a share ramp. Everything was "fill your boots". I didn't see it as share ramping, more a bit of fun with the stock market. We learned a very salutary lesson: you can't have fun with the stock market without it ending in the way that it did.'

Now, however, there was no love lost between Piers and his erstwhile protégés and he certainly wasn't going to waste time defending them. 'I think the Slickers have avoided most of the criticism that they probably should get for what they've done,' he observed. 'They know what they did, and they're City journalists – they should've been much more au fait with how it works than anybody else. [But] I totally held my hands up and said the managerial responsibility failed completely. Completely. And made mugs of all of us. After the PCC adjudication, what was clear to me afterwards was [that] it was bloody stupid of me to ever think that I could actively trade in the stock market and not at some stage come into conflict with the paper.'

Indeed, a month later, Sir Victor Blank stated that Piers was totally in the clear and, once more, everyone attempted to move on.

Labour won the 2001 election and, as the *Mirror* was the populist Labour-supporting newspaper, yet again Piers looked to be in the right place at the right time, although he issued a strong warning that the paper would be a 'critical friend'. But several months later, the September 11 atrocity took place, in which four planes were hijacked by terrorists and flown into the Twin Towers of New York's World Trade Center and the Pentagon in Washington, while the fourth crashed in a field in Stoneycreek Township. It would be wrong to make such an appalling act of carnage the backdrop to one man's life but, even so, the terrorist attacks set in place a train of events that would one day bring Piers down. On the day itself, he had been recuperating in bed after a back operation, but, as the scenes began to be played out on television, he decided that he'd rested enough and returned to his office.

'I was at home in Sussex recuperating from a bad back when I got the news,' he recalled, as all the editors on duty at the time were asked to recount their experiences. 'I switched on the TV in time to see the plane hitting the second tower. I immediately decided to drive to the office but, with the distraction of the news coming in, I got lost a couple of times despite knowing the route so well. I was concerned that we might have to evacuate Canary Wharf [the *Mirror*'s home] too and thank goodness we didn't. The news desk, everybody, acted phenomenally well.'

Shortly after the atrocity, the West began an offensive that continues to this day. The first proper military reaction was the invasion of Afghanistan, where the terrorists responsible – al-Qaeda and its head, Osama bin Laden – were hiding. In the shock and horror of the immediate aftermath of the attacks, the instinctive reaction was towards jingoism. Piers, however, responded far more thoughtfully than anyone might have expected.

It may have had something to do with the couple of years he had just endured. He had all but been dubbed a crook in light of the City Slickers' scandal and, what's more, there had been some ridicule directed towards him for the way his marriage had fallen apart. He was still a young man and a formidable operator but, for all that, Piers was unaccustomed to quite the level of abuse he'd been subjected to in recent years and may well have seen this as a chance to redeem himself. Whatever the reason, he declared publicly that he intended to make the *Mirror* a more 'serious' paper; no more was its agenda to be dominated by celebrities and reality TV, from now on, he would be tackling the issues that were important in this world.

'Could we still be splashing on this story in a year's time? Quite possibly,' said Piers, although that statement proved to be a little optimistic. (At the time of writing, nine years has elapsed and not only is Afghanistan still front-page news, but the complete lack of resolution means that Piers – pretty much uniquely among newspaper editors at the time – might have been right.) 'We could be in the middle of something which lasts five years and it may be that that gives the *Mirror* a unique opportunity to realign itself back with its heritage – the people's paper. I'm unashamedly populist – I have no problem putting Barrymore on the front page if he's talking about somebody dying in his swimming pool [but] there are a lot of bright, young people coming in to buy the paper to read about this inane, cretinous television we all got consumed by [*Big Brother*] and it was tempting to keep hammering at it as the main news of the day. I don't want to go back to that. It doesn't mean we won't do cultural phenomena and celebrities, but we're now heading for more of a *Mail*-style front page, where the main event on page one is a serious story.'

And so he began his new, serious take on the news, putting American politicians on the front page and demanding everyone involved be held to account. Over at the *Sun*, David Yelland was unimpressed; if anything, the war of words between himself and Piers had intensified in recent years and both were quick to rubbish anything the other had anything to do with.

'Self-congratulatory rubbish,' Yelland declared. 'It makes me chuckle to see Morgan reinvent himself as a serious journalist. It's easy if you edit a mass-market tabloid, like I do and Piers does – one of the few things we have in common – to get a lot of kudos if you splash with heavy stories. But the paper exists for readers, not media commentators.'

Now the feud between the two men was becoming pretty vicious, and the *Sun* stated that anyone opposing the War was a traitor. 'What the *Mirror* has done is nothing short of treachery,' it insisted. 'They questioned our forces as they were engaged in action. They poured scorn on our prime minister at a moment of grave danger for all of us.'

In turn, the *Mirror* responded by declaring that enemies of free speech were the real traitors and for good measure ran a picture of David Yelland alongside Hitler, Stalin and Osama bin Laden. Altogether, it was pretty nasty stuff.

Of course, none of this would have mattered if the new stance was proving popular with readers, but it was not the case. All the newspapers saw an increase in sales following September 11, as is usual after such a huge news story. In the months afterwards, when everything started to get back to normal, the *Mirror* wasn't doing anything like so well. Circulation was falling, and, while Piers was very enthusiastic about his newfound serious stance, the readers didn't agree: a balance had to be found between what was undoubtedly the biggest story of a generation and the celebrity fare that keeps *Mirror* readers happy – and it just wasn't happening.

Not that the paper had totally abandoned its interest in the world of celebrity. In late 2001, the news broke that actress Elizabeth Hurley was pregnant by American film producer Steve Bing, who publicly abandoned her as soon as the story became public. In the event, the *Mirror* came down on him like a tonne of bricks, publishing among much else his phone number. Bing promptly sued.

The case involving Naomi Campbell and infringement of privacy finally came to court: amid an enormous amount of publicity, Campbell won – although the fact that she was awarded just £3,500 in damages rather took the shine off the victory (plus a further £200,000 in costs). The judge actually accused her of lying under oath, while the *Mirror* fought back in typical style. In the wake of the judgment,

Piers was scathing. 'If Naomi Campbell wants to crack open the champagne, she might consider the prospect of getting a knock on the door from police over two matters,' he declared. 'One, she's been a regular Class-A drug abuser for many years, which is a serious offence. Two, she's lied under oath, which is perjury and could mean several years in prison. She's won £3,500, which is an embarrassingly small sum. One of her colleagues said supermodels don't get out of bed for £10,000. So she won't even get enough to pull back the bedclothes, which makes it even more ludicrous. You can get £4,000–£5,000 if a hairdresser damages your hair. She must be having a bad hair day.'

This was a typical blustering performance, but it concealed deeper worries. For a start, Piers' personal life was far from resolved. He was separated but not divorced, with a lot of uncertainty still in the background. Also, the *Mirror* was not finding its newly serious stance an unqualified success. Though widely considered a brilliant editor, Piers' normally golden touch had become a little tarnished of late. Had he but known it, a train of events had been set in motion that would finally see him catapulted out of the industry he had known and loved for so long, and set him on the path towards becoming a household name.

CHAPTER NINE
KING OF FEUDS

Both publicly and privately, it had been a tumultuous period – and was about to become even more so. Piers continued to be highly rated by his peers – in 2002, he was awarded Editor of the Year in the UK Press Awards for the second year running – but he was still in the news almost as much as he was reporting on it. And, although many liked to compare him to his erstwhile mentor and editor Kelvin MacKenzie, in that both were the most high-profile editors of their generation, the fact was that Kelvin, though he raised eyebrows, ruffled feathers and the rest of it, had never been caught up in a share imbroglio, unlike Piers. His protégé was treading a fine line and it wouldn't be too long before he finally overstepped the mark.

By now, Piers was becoming known for his feuds. The first, of course, had been with Ian Hislop, editor of *Private Eye*, which had rumbled on ever since that appearance on *Have I Got News For You* all those years ago. In the magazine, Piers was regularly referred to as 'Piers Moron'. In turn, he responded by running a feature in the *Mirror* called 'Gnomegate' (a reference to the mythical Lord Gnome, the so-called proprietor of *Private Eye*), in which he requested dirt on Hislop's private life. Interestingly enough, despite dark hints about taxes, nothing was ever forthcoming. 'We did have stuff, but tragically I got sacked before we could use it,' admitted Piers in an interview after leaving the *Mirror*, before revealing that it was completely untrue. 'OK, we couldn't find anything on him. That was the most shattering discovery about Hislop – he is as boring as he seems.'

No slouch when it came to defending himself, Hislop reacted with total disdain. 'It's all rather pathetic, really,' he told the *Observer*. 'He launched the campaign out of pure personal pique. He made a fool of himself on *Have I Got News For You*, which he was very embarrassed about. He was furious that we had written about, in particular, the share dealing. So he is touchy about his personal life, which is fairly extraordinary coming from a man who edited the *News Of The World*. He does this thing about: "Ooh, these people, they can dish it out but they can't take it." But I can take it. The man who can't is Piers, who devoted huge resources at the *Mirror* and doorstepped me, had journalists in my village and went on Friends Reunited to find everyone I've ever met. It wasn't fun, it wasn't a laugh, it was a very expensive and vindictive campaign to try and deflect criticism of himself. I think he thought he could get the *Eye* to stop writing about him, and it didn't work. The mountains, being in labour, bringing forth the ridiculous mouse…' Hislop's quote from Horace was just his way of saying that Piers had put a great deal of effort into something which yielded nothing.

Hislop went on to nominate Piers to go into Room 101, on the show of the same name, where guests could banish all the things they disliked most. However, he was rejected for being 'too toxic'.

In recent years, for unspecified reasons (possibly the fact that he was now a bona fide celebrity rather than a hack), Piers seemed to tire of feuding with Hislop and publicly announced he was done. 'The war is over. I'm officially calling an end to hostilities, at least from my end. I'm sure it won't stop him carrying on his "Piers Moron" stuff,' he declared.

'Is that an armistice or an unconditional surrender?' asked Hislop.

And the second feud, obviously, was with David Yelland. There really was a visceral dislike between the two men that had nothing to do with the fact that they were editing rival newspapers and the situation with Marina Hyde only made it worse. She and Piers always denied the affair but they were undoubtedly close in some way and this was referred to when Yelland gave an interview to *GQ* magazine, in which he was asked about the email exchange.

'We have three boxes of emails,' said Yelland. 'They are explosive, but I've never leaked them. They could destroy him, but I won't leak them because they could destroy his kids.' And if that wasn't enough, he added that Piers had a 'schoolboy, lavatory sense of humour, with an extremely nasty edge'.

Meanwhile, Piers refused to take all this lying down; there was 'chronic insecurity' at the *Sun*, he declared. 'They delighted in embarrassing me, and in being quite destructive to a friend and to my personal life. I think of Yelland sitting there with his operatives, salivating over them [the emails] and it makes me quite sick.'

'What worries me is that our relationship will define us as editors. People will think of us as the bald one and the corrupt one,' said Yelland (who happened to be bald).

'He calls me "corrupt". He can't prove it, but I can prove he's bald,' was Piers' response.

Matters came to a head at the UK Press Awards, where Piers directed a four-letter-word-strewn rant at Yelland, after the latter attempted to offer him congratulations on winning the award. 'Fuck off, you c**t! No, I *mean* it, I *really* mean it – fuck off, you *bald* c**t!' he said.

Onlookers, including Yelland's wife Tania, appeared to be genuinely shocked, although Piers remained defiant about his tirade.

'I don't like David Yelland,' he commented afterwards. 'He was the one who said that he had information on my private life that would destroy my children. How would *you* feel about someone like that?'

The main issue seemed to be Marina Hyde, but there was something else at play as well; Yelland was, after all, editor of the *Sun*, not only the rival to the *Mirror* but also the newspaper on which Piers had learned to ply his trade. Both men had come up through the ranks, but in a very different way – while Piers had been a show-business reporter, Yelland made his name through financial journalism, which was one reason why his appointment had been greeted with some surprise. Many suspected Piers felt the job should have gone to him and this was the real cause of his animosity. Certainly, he began attacking Yelland from the moment he got the job in 1998, and well before anything to do with Hyde appeared on the scene.

'Piers could never say he hates David because he got the job, but there is no doubt that's why it all started,' observed one erstwhile colleague. 'Piers was thinking, there's that bald lad who's not as good a journalist as me and he's got the top job and I've ended up with the second [now the third, behind the *Sun* and *Daily Mail* in terms of sales] paper.'

Associates of Yelland agreed. 'David got what Piers had always wanted, that's what really pisses him off,' said one.

In the wake of the Press Awards, Piers appeared to have a complete rethink and sent out an email to *Mirror* staff. 'The war with the *Sun*, and Mr Yelland, is now officially over,' he announced. 'It seems churlish to intrude into their private grief at this difficult time [just one UK Press Award] so there will be no more references to them in the *Mirror* with immediate effect.'

And he was not the only one to make conciliatory noises.

Apart from attempting to offer congratulations, Yelland had also shown total support for the *Mirror*'s stance in the case with Naomi Campbell and, while he might have been expected to do so, given that it involved press freedom as much as anything else, the fact is he still chose to do so.

Campbell actually admitted to lying in court about the extent of her drug use, while at the same time there was widespread contempt about the fact that she had ended up playing the 'race card'. *Mirror* columnist Sue Carroll had recently dubbed her a 'chocolate soldier' in reference to the fact that, after pledging support to the animal welfare group PETA, she had gone on to pose in furs. Despite no evidence of racism whatsoever, Naomi decided this was a reference to the colour of her skin (rather than, as was plainly meant, a reference to her being a useless defender of a cause), something the judge also commented on. In the end, she won her case on narrow grounds indeed, those of 'data protection' and the 'duty of confidence' of Narcotics Anonymous towards those seeking help. She was not granted a larger award because the judge held against her a record of 'dissembling' – only the revelation about Narcotics Anonymous was wrong.

'OK, so what the judge said was that, if we'd simply run a story saying that she's a lying, druggie model who should be kicked off the catwalk, we'd have been all right,' Piers rather witheringly commented afterwards. 'The only thing we did wrong was to put her story in a sympathetic light and say that she was seeking treatment. I do believe in a degree of privacy but it is dependent on that person's behaviour. She [Naomi Campbell] was breaking the law. If she was a burglar going to Burglars Anonymous, would you say that we didn't have the right to reveal she'd been out housebreaking?'

David Yelland, it seemed, was in agreement. 'Naomi Campbell is a liar, a loser and coward. In fact, she could be arrested and jailed for perjury next time she comes to Britain. She is also a drug abuser and a thoroughly nasty piece of work,' observed a leader in the *Sun* in the wake of the case. 'So has she really "won" her case against the *Mirror*? No, she has not. In fact, the *Mirror* won. So did all newspapers. And so did all readers. Campbell's character lies in ruins. She has received a mere £3,500 in damages. She has had her private life dragged through the courts. And she may even end up in the clink. Some victory! This obnoxious woman didn't even have the guts to turn up to court yesterday.

'And what on earth is a judge doing telling a *Mirror* columnist what language to use? What right does he have to say the words "chocolate soldier" are "racist"? What is he: a bewigged sub-editor? Come off it. Celebrities have too much power, not too little. They are often weak, useless, arrogant bullies whom the press has a duty to expose. If the legal establishment wishes to gather its tanks on Fleet Street's lawn we will fire back. Even if it means standing shoulder to shoulder with our most bitter rival.'

So, did the mutual stance last? No. There was too much

personal antipathy between the two for any real bridges to be built (Yelland as much as Piers). In April 2002, the *Mirror* relaunched, with various new heavyweight journalists such as Jonathan Friedland and Christopher Hitchens on board to fit in with the paper's new image, aimed slightly more upmarket than before. At the same time, it also ditched the trademark red masthead. Yelland lost no time in making his position felt; he declared his immediate rival was 'as second rate now as it has ever been'.

Indeed, he sent an email to *Sun* staff that was highly critical of the new-look *Mirror*. 'THE DAY they relaunched was the lowest Wednesday sale for the *Mirror* in its entire history,' he wrote. 'The *Mirror* has, in reality, surrendered the Red Top market to us after a 32-year fight. They have made a strategic mistake of huge proportions. THE Mirror's claim to be a serious paper is simply an empty promise. It is very easy to SAY you are serious, but to BE serious you have to UNDERSTAND the big issues. They do not.'

Yelland was suffering from 'major psychological problems', declared Piers. And then, if that were not enough, a month later, the *Mirror* took out an advertisement in the *Press Gazette* with a footballer bearing Yelland's face doubled up in pain as the ball hits him in the groin; underneath the heading NEWSPAPER WAR UPDATE was the line: 'How much pain can one man take?'

'I said I wouldn't attack him again in the paper – I never

Piers with Celia Walden at the opening of Gordon Ramsay's Maze at the Marriott in 2005. The pair got married in 2010.

A star-studded evening. At the BAFTA television awards with Harry Hill and Alesha Dixon.

Morgan's got talent! Part of Piers' reinvention as a TV personality came with his appointment as a judge on ITV's *Britain's Got Talent*.

Above: With fellow judges Amanda Holden and Simon Cowell.

Below: Meeting hopefuls at the Glasgow leg of the auditions for the show.

Piers' television career continues to go from strength to strength with his *Piers Morgan On …* documentary series for ITV.

This Page: Visiting Hollywood and meeting the Osbournes in LA.

Opposite Page. *Above left*: In front of the world's tallest building in Dubai.

Above right: Speaking to Simply Red's Mick Hucknall in opulent Monaco.

Below: Checking out the plush residences in Sandbanks, Dorset.

Above: Piers proves he's game when taking part in *Celebrity Apprentice*.

Below left: Taking part in a charity cricket match with Richie Richardson.

Below right: Friends again. Piers and Naomi Campbell put aside their differences for Fashion Relief.

Piers and Celia Walden's wedding party in July 2010.

Above left: The happy couple cut the cake.

Above right: Lord Sugar and his wife, Ann, were among the wedding party guests.

Below left: The groom with Sarah Brown.

Below right: Amanda Holden and Christine Bleakley.

Piers cracks it Stateside. An advertisement for *Piers Morgan Tonight*.
He took over Larry King's slot at the beginning of 2011.

said anything about whacking the little twat elsewhere,' was Piers' cool remark.

In 2003, David Yelland left the *Sun* after a five-year period to be replaced by Rebekah Wade, with whom Piers got on considerably better and for whom he had a good deal more respect. Yelland himself ended up working in the business world (in financial PR), for which, in truth, many felt he was better suited. He eventually admitted to prolonged alcoholism while editing the *Sun*, and subsequently wrote a children's novel. The very public war between himself and Piers was over when he stepped down, but it's fair to say no love has ever been lost between the two of them.

Unsurprisingly, given the circumstances, Piers went on to feud with Naomi Campbell for a while. The *Mirror* appealed and won the case, following which Naomi took it to the House of Lords, where she won again.

'This is a good day for lying, drug-abusing prima donnas who want to have their cake with the media and the right to then shamelessly guzzle it with their Cristal champagne,' was how Piers summed it up. 'Five senior judges found for the *Mirror* throughout the various hearings in this case, four for Naomi Campbell. Yet she wins. If ever there was a less deserving case for creating what is effectively a backdoor privacy law, it would be Ms Campbell, but that's showbiz.'

Campbell herself did not hold back on what she thought about the case. 'Miss Campbell is delighted by today's verdict by the House of Lords,' her lawyer, Keith Schilling, said in a statement. 'It is not only a vindication for her personally but, more importantly, represents a real advantage for the rights of people to maintain important elements of their privacy, particularly when related to therapy and people who need to have treatment. Throughout these proceedings, neither Miss Campbell nor anyone in her legal team has ever questioned the ability of the press to report the fact that she had a problem with drugs and that she had previously misled the press about these drugs. By taking the Court of Appeal's judgment to the House of Lords, at no small level of stress to herself, she was simply determined to fight the cause of an individual's basic rights to be left alone to receive therapy without the glare of the media spotlight, which can self-evidently be harmful to the necessary treatment. But this is not a blow for so-called freedom of the press nor is it a charter just to protect celebrities; if anything this new law underpins the integrity of the media by ensuring the freedom of people in therapy to receive the treatment they need and for them to express themselves openly and in confidence without fear of media intrusion.'

And so it went on, until the relationship changed dramatically, so much so that they are – if not exactly friends – a good deal more tolerant of one another than previously. Matters changed dramatically in 2007, three years after Piers had left the *Mirror*, when Dylan Jones, editor of *GQ* magazine, arranged for him to interview

Naomi in a mutual publicity coup. He described the result as 'incendiary' and he was probably right.

Piers started as he meant to go on. 'Right, Naomi, when the *Mirror* lost its infamous court battle the first time around, I stood on the steps of the High Court and called you a "lying, drug-abusing, egotistical, pampered, self-deluded prima donna",' he began.

'Yes, you did,' said Naomi, who was to come across considerably better in this interview than she usually did.

'Would you debate any of those?'

'Er, I'm not self-deluded.'

Campbell went on to say that she regretted her chronic lateness, first took drugs when she was twenty-four years old and had indeed become an addict.

She also put up a spirited defence of her right to privacy: 'I don't think anyone should be exposed for taking drugs. That person is ill, they are sick.' And she was of the view that drugs should never be legalised, and not unreasonably pointed out that, in many cases, alcohol is just as harmful; she also put up a reasonable explanation for drugs in the world of modelling.

She went on to speak up for her fellow model Kate Moss, who had been exposed in the *Mirror* for taking drugs (Piers was long gone by that time). 'I was upset that she was treated that way,' she said. 'She is hurting herself and, when it's exposed, she doesn't have the space or time to help herself because everyone is looking at her. It's hard.'

Most of all, though, she was completely open about why

she was being interviewed by Piers Morgan, of all people – the man who many felt had gone too far. 'Because I wanted to talk to you,' she explained. 'A lot of my friends didn't want me to do this and I haven't told some of them that I am doing it because they were so upset about what I went through with the court case. But I don't hold grudges, Piers, and I feel stronger and I'm in a different place in my life. And I understand you were selling newspapers. But it did hurt, and you should know that.'

Nor would she accept his explanation that they were just trying to show the situation in a positive light.

They continued along the lines of a regular interview, with Naomi proving to be quite a sport, until the tables turned. Piers had not been warned of this in advance but, suddenly, she pulled out a large notebook and began interviewing him. He went along with it. After all, what else could he have done? The occasion had been a brilliant success and, from then on, the two were almost friends.

It certainly hadn't been like that with David Yelland, one of Piers' prime targets, although it must be said that Yelland was no statuesque supermodel. But Yelland was by no means the person with whom Piers had the biggest feud: that honour goes to Jeremy Clarkson, who at one point actually threw a punch at him. The trouble started in 2000, when Piers was given a picture of Jeremy kissing a woman other than his wife and chose to publish it. (Clarkson, incidentally, has it that the feud began when Piers approached him to leave the *Sun* and write for the

Mirror instead, but he turned him down.) However, the paper did not go particularly big on the story because, so Piers was later to say, Jeremy made a personal appeal to him to go easy – 'Look, Piers, I'm going to tell you something now: I'm not capable of having an affair, I'm not physically capable' – an allegation that came out a good deal later, when things became really nasty.

A year or so later, another picture of Jeremy kissing the same woman – a BBC employee – came to light, and this time the gloves really were off. Piers went big on the story, causing an enraged response from Clarkson that was played out in several chapters. The first came about in October 2003, when both were invited to take part in Concorde's last-ever flight. 'I hope I am sitting near Piers Morgan,' Jeremy told Simon Kelner, the editor of the *Independent*, the night before the flight. 'Then you'll have a story because I'm going to punch that little shit's lights out.' He very nearly managed it, too.

Afterwards, other members of the flight reported that 'banter' took place between them, but it was more than that; as soon as Jeremy set eyes on Piers, he snarled, 'Let's sort it out now,' as he rolled up his sleeves. Given the plane was about to take off, it wasn't really practical; instead, Jeremy contented himself with pouring the contents of his champagne into Piers' lap. (Or, according to some sources, his glass of water.)

The next occasion was in March 2004. This time, the two were at the British Press Awards, always a pretty riotous affair, at the Park Lane Hilton in London. Drink flowed, and, in the early hours, Jeremy let his temper get the better of him. This time, he did lash out, punching Piers three times and knocking him to the ground.

But Piers made light of it all. 'They were three pitiful blows. I have had bigger drubbings from my three-year-old son,' he declared. 'There has been a simmering volcanic rage since we published the photos of Clarkson. I upset him at the Press Awards when I suggested his wife would be happier if he did not embrace other women.'

'He's won,' snapped Clarkson. 'I've hurt my finger and he's fine.'

Piers was then asked by Lynn Barber in the *Observer* whether it wasn't a bit unkind to have gone public with the remark about Clarkson not being physically capable. 'Ah, diddums! Poor little diddums!' Piers retorted. 'You'll start telling me I should feel sorry for Ian Hislop next. Do me a favour! These guys dish it out – they just don't like it up 'em. If Clarkson wants to punch me, that's his problem. I'd just like to say through the annals of this august organ that, if he does it again, especially when I've had a few, and now I'm not in a position of any proper responsibility, the phrase "sack of potatoes" springs to mind.'

Nor was this the end of it. 'I still have a two-inch scar from his ring down the right side of my forehead,' Piers revealed sometime later. 'Never could stand jewellery on a man.'

'Piers Morgan, you are an arsehole,' was Clarkson's response.

Another of Piers' feuds is with the journalist AA Gill, who, coincidentally or not, is close friends with Jeremy Clarkson. As so often with these spats, the origins are shrouded in mystery, with both sides claiming different stories, but what was certainly true was that, as Piers' television career really began to take off in 2003, Gill – a television critic – was never slow to pour bile into his reviews.

Rather mysteriously, Gill's girlfriend Nicola Formby appeared to be involved. Also a journalist, she had taken Piers out to lunch to interview him before, for some reason, showing him a series of extremely provocative pictures of herself.

'You could see everything and the poses were explicit,' said Piers. 'Ms Formby sprawled here, Ms Formby's legs akimbo there, Ms Formby thrusting her bottom everywhere. She obviously thinks she's an absolute sex kitten, but I fear the mists of time have taken their toll a little too much.'

Given this, perhaps unsurprisingly AA Gill did not find it within himself to be generous to Piers. Several years later, he went on to present a television show with Amanda Platell, which Gill branded 'jaw-droppingly grim' and 'huggably appalling'.

'Oh, dreadful little man, absolutely dreadful! Disgusting,' said Piers in return.

The incident with the photographs simply wasn't true, added AA Gill, at which point he was asked why he didn't sue. 'Oh, because I'm never going to sue anyone, ever. I think Piers Morgan is a pretty objectionable self-publicist, but he has no room in my head – I know what the truth is.'

He didn't let it go, either: his role as a television reviewer afforded him plenty of opportunity to take a pop at Piers any time he liked. Of the ITV1 talent competition *Britain's Got Talent*, he wrote, 'The only pleasure is watching the skin-crawling Piers Morgan, Gore-Tex man, impervious to any emotion or sensitivity. He seems to have learned human as a second language, possibly from Derren Brown. He is by far and away the weirdest act in the room. His descent (ascent?) from editor of the *Mirror* to ventriloquist's invigilator is, it must be said, one of the most comforting comeuppances of contemporary celebrity. He kept asking awful kiddie-party turns if they thought they were the sort of thing the Queen wanted to see when you knew the one person the Queen would abdicate rather than sit next to was asking the question.'

No love lost there, then.

Then there were the other feuds, less public but nonetheless protracted. Piers and Cherie Blair famously loathed one another; he also feuded periodically with Carol Vorderman, Robbie Coltrane and Madonna. Later, after he was named Larry King's replacement on CNN, Piers announced that he wouldn't be having Madonna on the show 'because she's too old now and we have Lady Gaga'. Madonna responded in style by saying she had no idea who Piers was, but she was a big fan of Lady Gaga.

'All a bit of a laugh, really – part of the caricature,'

chortled Piers of his feuds. According to him, Jonathan Ross is a 'talentless little fuckwit', while Ross himself described Piers as a 'grotesque talent vacuum'. 'I hate that chat-show thing, with people plugging their music or their movie in seven-minute slots,' insisted Piers, as he himself started to become more of a chat-show host. 'People find them boring. That's why Ross's ratings are down on last year, plus the issues he had with [Russell] Brand. He can't even leer over actresses any more. He's lost his confidence and you can see it in his show.'

In a statement to an interviewer after he left the *Mirror*, Piers admitted he would like to edit the *Sunday Times* because 'The idea of firing Clarkson and AA Gill could be irresistible. Put that in.'

'I like waging feuds,' he said in 2009. 'They get me going and make me perform better. I don't start them, but I always finish them. I miss it [from working on newspapers]: on newspapers every day is a feud – all editors need one to get by.'

In truth, though, it's hard to tell why Piers was involved in quite so many feuds as he was. There was the case of professional rivalry (David Yelland), upsetting people by reporting on their private lives (Jeremy Clarkson) and then the good old desire to drum up publicity (Madonna); then there has been the public reconciliation (Naomi Campbell) and life-long antipathy (it's hard to imagine he'll be making it up with AA Gill any time soon). Above all, there has always been the desire to entertain.

Although he started feuding almost as soon as he entered journalism, sometimes to the bemusement of *Mirror* readers (who must have wondered why they were reading so much about the editor of the *Sun*), it probably didn't occur to Piers at first just how much entertainment value these feuds could attract and, as time went on, such proved to be the case. Meanwhile, he was increasingly drawn to the world of entertainment; he might have started out as a showbiz reporter but he was increasingly being sucked into the real thing himself. He was still a newspaper editor with a determination to keep the *Mirror* reporting on serious news – an obsession that would ultimately land him in big trouble – but increasingly he was appearing on television, too, although at that stage it seemed more like a sideline than the direction in which his future lay.

His TV appearances were now becoming more accomplished. That early foray into *Have I Got News For You* hadn't worked out so well, but he was learning that television – the medium of spectacle and noise – is very different to newspapers, the medium of the written word. Piers proved a very fast learner, one who got better with every passing day.

And so in 2003, while he was still beavering away at the *Mirror*, he was given his first proper television series. At the time, no one expected this to be anything more than a one-off, but with hindsight it's clear that it was to pave the way to his future, just as much as his ultimate sacking from the *Mirror*.

Piers Morgan, television superstar, was on his way.

CHAPTER TEN

TABLOID TALES

At the start of 2003, it seemed very much to be business as usual; Piers was managing to maintain both his own profile and that of the *Mirror*. He gleefully greeted the announcement that David Yelland was leaving the *Sun* to attend business school in the US with the words: 'I wish him every success with his schoolwork.' By then, Piers had been editing the *Mirror* for seven years and he'd now seen off a second editor at the *Sun* – he might perhaps be forgiven for feeling somewhat pleased with himself.

Rebekah Wade took over and hostilities between the two papers immediately dampened down. Ultimately to become chief executive of News International, which owned the *Sun* and its various sister papers, she was a far more obvious choice of editor than Yelland had ever been. Meanwhile, it was all change at the *Mirror*, with Sylvia 'Sly' Bailey taking over as managing director of the Mirror Group. The rumour was that Piers was not best pleased about this, not least because his attempt to reposition the *Mirror* as a serious newspaper had not been wholly successful. There were tensions about the direction it should take next.

The annual hugely successful Pride of Britain Awards took place, but darker clouds now gathered in the background, too. Ever since the terrorist atrocity of September 11, there had been increased murmurings that the West was about to attack Iraq. Dictator Saddam Hussein was said to have amassed Weapons of Mass Destruction, with warnings that he could use them on Britain with as little as forty-five minutes' notice. Calls to attack were coming mainly from the US, but British Prime Minister Tony Blair was sounding increasingly hawkish. Most of the written media backed a war that was by now seen as almost inevitable, but the *Mirror* refused to do so: right from the start, it warned that the Iraq War would be a disaster and Piers was to pay a heavy price for this stance – even if, years later, he would appear to have been proved right. The War duly began in March 2003, whereupon the *Mirror* warned that it would be a mistake. It maintained a highly critical stance, which was to prove unpopular with the readers – the thought being that British newspapers should support British soldiers at war – and led directly to Piers' demise.

Indeed, he soon recognised that he'd got the mood of the public wrong. At this stage, the paper was running front-page photos of civilian casualties with the headline STILL ANTI-WAR? YES, BLOODY RIGHT WE ARE. But the readers hated it: circulation began to fall sharply, prompting a hasty editorial rethink. 'We no longer address the anti-war issue on the front page, we just tell the story as it happens,' Piers told one interviewer (he was always good at owning up when he got something wrong). 'I felt that we could carry on being pretty aggressively critical on the front page and we caught a bit of a cold, to be honest. I personally slightly misjudged the way that you could be attitudinal on the front page in the way that we were once the War actually started. A fascinating thing happened, something I have not experienced in ten years editing papers – I have never seen such a switch in public opinion.'

And there was even praise for what Rebekah Wade was now doing over at the *Sun*. 'You can see a much more aggressive approach, more gung-ho on the War. It's not my cup of tea, but I think for her readership it's bang on,' declared Piers.

Of course, it helped that he had a brother in the Army (who apparently also told him to cool the negativity), but, ominously, several American journalists had recently been fired for digitally altering pictures of the War and Piers was asked if he'd do the same. 'We've had a few incidents here and even the *Guardian* had one on Budget Day once,' he said. 'There's always a temptation to "clean up" a picture, which can be done very quickly on a computer but we now have a strict policy where we don't tamper with pictures... except where we're doing so deliberately to make them entertaining and we now acknowledge we've done it. Given the power of computers now, not saying you've altered a picture is unethical.'

Printing false ones could land you in a spot of bother, too. But it wasn't all about the War, as Piers was becoming involved in some very different projects, too. As one of Britain's most high-profile editors and someone who also knew the world of celebrity inside out, the previous autumn he had been approached by the BBC to make a television series about the relationship between fame and the media. It was to end up in an interview format, a precursor to what he would be doing in ITV's *Piers Morgan's Life Stories*, and he was certainly in a position to pull in the truly famous. Here is Piers on the type of people who took part: 'Victoria Beckham and Jade Goody fell into the "Yes, we've had a lot of rubbish written about us, but it doesn't really bother us and it's all a bit of a game, isn't it?" category. Heather Mills McCartney and Paul Burrell made up the "Bemused and rather hurt Fleet Street hero to zero for no really sensible reason" brigade. And Peter Mandelson and Anthea Turner placed themselves squarely in the "We're gonna chew you up, spit you out and then dance on your 'orrible little graves" camp.'

The series, which began in April 2003, was an immediate hit. Both viewers and critics liked it (although the latter refused to become too fulsome, possibly because they were on rival papers), and Piers unquestionably turned out to have a knack for drawing people out. After all, that's what he had started off doing, back in the days of 'Bizarre'

– which is when he also began creating his impressive contacts book. He managed to keep making the headlines, not least when he interviewed Peter Mandelson and the latter revealed that he feared his second sacking would destroy him. (For the record, this did not prove the case.) Then it was Heather Mills' turn and she railed against being branded a 'gold digger'. Following this, Paul Burrell hinted that Diana's death was more than just an accident. Every one of these and many more made the headlines; Piers clearly maintained a feel for a good story, even if the medium had now changed.

Back at the *Mirror*, however, things were not going so well. At the Trinity Mirror annual meeting, chairman Sir Victor Blank commented that Piers was 'not at the moment on the way out'. Though he also praised him for being a good editor, this was hardly a ringing endorsement, for the problem was Piers' increasingly strident campaign against the War in Iraq. His stance was losing readers hand over fist, not least because it felt slightly unpatriotic, but to have changed tack now would be a public humiliation for him. While there was unease, no one was exactly sure what to do.

There was now increasing speculation that Piers really could be on his way out – that 'serious' agenda wasn't helping things either – but he clung on and got on with the job. And he still had his triumphs: an interview with Tony Martin (the farmer who shot at two intruders in his home) made headlines around the country, and a letter from Princess Diana, in which she averred that a shadowy figure (who turned out to be Prince Charles) was planning to kill her in a car crash made headlines around the world. The *Mirror* then sent a reporter to work as a footman at Buckingham Palace for two months – a story that was published complete with pictures of the Queen's breakfast and the first day when US President George W. Bush stayed the night there – provoking a huge security row.

When Piers was causing ructions, setting the news agenda and getting himself and his paper talked about all the time, he was at his best, but the War in Iraq continued, and still the *Mirror* refused to budge on its stance. In the background, his relationship with Marina Hyde was beginning to peter out; it was a time of considerable stress. However, that television career was really beginning to take off: after his triumph at the BBC, Piers moved over to Channel 4, where he presented *The Importance of Being Famous*, a three-part series on the modern obsession with fame. This brought forward accusations of his having his cake and eating it; in print he was running a 'serious' newspaper, while on the screen he was enjoying a good nose around the lives of the rich and famous. Then there was the fact that he was becoming almost a celebrity himself, with a high profile that kept on growing. In fact, he was setting himself up for a huge career move, although no one – himself included – realised this at the time.

And then, at the beginning of May 2004, came the end of Piers' career as a tabloid editor. In the past, he had taken plenty of risks (and just about got away with them), but now he went a step too far. There had already been stories of American soldiers abusing prisoners in Iraq, and indeed some pretty horrific pictures to go with them. Now it seemed that British troops could be implicated, too. The *Mirror* received – and published – photos that it said came from two soldiers in the Queen's Lancashire Regiment, showing members of the Army in southern Iraq beating up an Iraqi prisoner. In an attack that went on for eight hours, the man's jaw was broken, his teeth smashed and he was urinated on before being dumped from a moving vehicle. The scenes were harrowing – but were they actually true?

'We've carried out extensive checks to establish the veracity of the photographs and have no doubts about their authenticity,' said a *Mirror* spokesman, but others weren't so sure. Doubts were cast on numerous elements of the scene: the gun a soldier was holding was the wrong sort of SA-80 rifle; the hat was also wrong, as was the truck in which all this was supposedly going on and, given what was said to be happening to the prisoner, he looked remarkably composed.

This was serious stuff: the War – which was becoming increasingly controversial, given no Weapons of Mass Destruction in Iraq had been found for the simple reason that they didn't exist – was still going on, and to allege this sort of abuse actually put British soldiers at risk. It also impugned their integrity at a time when they needed support from their fellow countrymen, not false claims.

Piers' anti-war campaign had been unpopular enough as it was, and running these pictures would have one of two outcomes: either validate everything he had been saying or prove to be the straw that broke the camel's back.

At the time, it was alleged that hundreds of such pictures had been taken and were being passed among British soldiers; there were rumours that the British Military Police were planning some arrests, too. The Ministry of Defence launched an investigation, which was made more difficult because, unlike in the American pictures, you couldn't see anyone's face. The victim himself was wearing a hood.

Naturally, the Queen's Lancashire Regiment was extremely concerned. Its former commander, Colonel David Black, spoke out publicly. There were just too many inconsistencies, he said, adding the soldiers would have been wearing helmets or a beret and not floppy hats; they would also have had a regiment identification flash and the rifle should have had a sling.

'What they're feeling at the moment is dismay that this has occurred, disgusted at the allegations that have been made and not a little bit angry that their good name has been dragged through the mud,' he commented. 'It's been a terrible shock to them. In fact, the Bedford MK – which appears in the photographs, as I gather – was not deployed by the Army to Iraq at all because of difficulties with local fuel; that vehicle can't operate with fuel that was available in Iraq. So obviously the photograph was probably not even taken in Iraq. It will make the present soldiers serving in Iraq, be they British or coalition, their job will be much more difficult and much more dangerous. So, no matter what the motive was originally, and I couldn't begin to speculate, it has muddied the situation desperately. It's a tragedy.'

Criticising the War was one thing, putting soldiers' lives at risk in an increasingly bloody battle quite another. As more and more military personnel began to express doubts about the authenticity of the pictures, calls for an inquiry escalated and a sense of unease began to settle in among *Mirror* staff, but Piers remained adamant the pictures were authentic and that the decision to publish was right.

It was 'outrageous and unlawful behaviour' which 'has been common knowledge among disgusted British servicemen in Basra for many months', he said. 'These two soldiers felt compelled to expose what went on because they believed it was fundamentally wrong and that it would inevitably be reported. Whether you are in favour of the War or against it, there is unanimity that this behaviour is unacceptable.'

It certainly would have been, had it actually happened, but now there was real room for doubt and senior *Mirror* executives were beginning to express concern. Meanwhile, Piers battled on. 'We would not have published if there was any doubt that what was being presented was true,' he insisted. And he would make 'no apology for exposing this outrageous and unlawful behaviour, which has been common knowledge among disgusted British servicemen in Basra for many months. Nor do we believe that there is any reason to think that these photographs have been faked in any way at all, given the powerful testimony we have received.'

But the die had been cast; Piers was now in serious trouble.

As the row mounted, Armed Forces Minister Adam Ingram was forced to address MPs, while Charles Kennedy – then Leader of the Liberal Democrats – warned that the pictures, true or false, would have a 'massive impact' across the Muslim and Arab world. Piers was called on to appear before the House of Commons Defence Select Committee. Matters were not helped by the fact that, over in the US, more (real) pictures of the torture of Iraqis by American soldiers were beginning to emerge at the notorious prison Abu Ghraib, and President Bush denounced the behaviour as 'abhorrent'. Back in the UK, Prime Minister Tony Blair talked of the 'wholly unacceptable' behaviour in the photos, but added, 'That's what we went to Iraq to get rid of, not to perpetuate; the vast bulk of British troops out there would also be horrified if any such incidents had taken place.'

It was in the midst of all this that Naomi Campbell finally won her case at the House of Lords, but Piers had much more to worry about than that, including increasing calls for his resignation if the pictures turned out to be fake. While he responded with all his usual bombast, the end was near. And it made no difference that the *Mirror* itself was in the headlines for no less than three reasons

– the Campbell case, the Buckingham Palace security row and now the Iraq abuse pictures – if Piers, as editor, couldn't prove that what he had printed was real, then he would find himself in serious trouble.

In what would turn out to be his last big interview as editor of the *Mirror*, Piers talked to the *Observer* about why he had published the pictures and his belief that they were genuine, as well as the allegation that he had put the lives of British soldiers at risk. 'You have to look at this as two separate issues,' he insisted. 'One is the issue of the veracity of these photographs, and the bigger issue is whether the events happened. I have no doubts that the abuse has been very widespread and very serious by these rogue elements and the testimony of Soldier C [who told the *Mirror* last week of ill treatment] is compelling and very significant. He didn't ask for or receive any payment. The Government and the British Army have had a week to verify or knock down these photographs, and they have been unable to do either.

'That shows we took every step we could [to check the pictures]. I believe there is nothing irresponsible in publishing if you are confident of your sources, you know they are who they say they are, you know they were in Iraq at that time and they are providing you with a welter of photographic evidence, not just what we published, showing what they were up to. They are very convincing, ordinary soldiers who felt they had to come forward. I resent the way it is now assumed by the media that these must be fakes purely because last weekend was a long bank holiday and people have nothing else to do but wheel on ex-military guys and say, "I don't think those shoelaces look right." That is not good enough.'

As for the almost complete lack of identifying marks, he remained bullish. 'They've clearly gone to some lengths to ensure that if these pictures ever become public there is no identification. That is a simple, logical explanation.' And then there was the fact that his own brother was serving in Iraq. 'I won't go into what he thinks or feels about any of this because that is a matter for him, and I wouldn't compromise him,' he insisted. 'But that should show people how carefully I have thought about this and the consequences. I have a lot of military people in my family and I have taken soundings. What really irritates me is the allegation that we have caused massive problems for the troops on the ground in Basra. That is completely untrue. I say to people like Nicholas Soames that what has put our soldiers' lives at risk is a) waging this war in the first place, and the *Mirror*'s position on that is well known, and b) the behaviour of this rogue element of the Queen's Lancashire Regiment. It is that that has caused the problem, not this belated exposure in this country.'

It was to be his last hurrah – in that particular role, at least. On 13 May 2004, Adam Ingram stated the type of truck featured in the pictures had never been in Iraq and the pictures were plainly false. The next day, Piers had no choice but to resign. Following his resignation, the *Mirror* issued a grovelling apology, saying it had been 'the subject of a calculated and malicious hoax'.

Meanwhile, the Mirror Group commented, 'The Board of Trinity Mirror has decided that it would be inappropriate for Piers Morgan to continue in his role as editor of the *Daily Mirror* and he will therefore be stepping down with immediate effect. There is now sufficient evidence to suggest that these pictures are fakes and that the *Daily Mirror* has been the subject of a calculated and malicious hoax. The *Daily Mirror* therefore apologises unreservedly for publishing the pictures and deeply regrets the reputation damage done to the QLR [Queen's Lancashire Regiment] and the Army in Iraq.'

The *Mirror* printed a huge front page: SORRY ... WE WERE HOAXED.

There was a palpable sense of shock when Piers stood down. Love him or loathe him (and there was no shortage in both camps), for more than a decade now, he had been an impressive player on Fleet Street. A character and sometimes a chancer, he was hugely talented and had had a great input into the fabric of the nation. Whatever others may have thought about him, it is telling that those who worked for him tended to be some of his greatest admirers and he was extremely popular among the staff. Of course, alongside the incessant feuding, he'd made plenty of enemies along the way – no national newspaper editor can do otherwise – and there were plenty of others gloating about his fate. The situation was also in some ways a let-out for the *Mirror*. Although no one had been in any doubt that Piers was a class act, his anti-war stance had proved massively unpopular with readers and, while Mirror Group bosses would have found it difficult to get rid of him on those grounds, it was a good chance to start afresh. Now they could tone down the anti-war rhetoric without loss of face to anyone, for Piers was stepping down not on the grounds of his dislike of the War but because he'd made a terrible mistake.

To begin with, at least, it was unclear what he would do next. He was to negotiate a very healthy pay-off from the *Mirror* (and he had been extremely well paid for many years by then, so money wasn't an immediate problem – although he did have an estranged wife and three children to support). But he was not yet forty, and the loss of status and power came as an enormous shock. His mentor Kelvin MacKenzie has spoken of his own surprise at the number of unreturned calls after he stopped being an editor and Piers now began to discover the same thing. A national newspaper editor is one of the most powerful people in the country – there are a handful of them, as opposed to over 600 MPs – and Piers had proved adept at setting the agenda over and over again. Without a newspaper, he could no longer do that and, as such, no one was all that interested in what he had to say.

And the change in lifestyle was immense, too. As an editor, every minute of the day was accounted for; as well as putting the newspaper together, there was the constant round of lunches, drinks and dinners with the movers and shakers of this world: award ceremonies, black-tie dinners, the works... Suddenly, he was at a loose end – and very unexpectedly, too. There were no demands on his time and he could come and go as he pleased. It was a new sensation, and an unpleasant one at that; Piers does not have the kind of personality to make him curl up in a heap when things go wrong but this came as very much a shock.

As he himself told it in later years, he did a number of things. A slight and uncharacteristic aimlessness entered the proceedings: the odd boozy lunch because he had nothing else to do, afternoons spent idling as it was not clear what would come next. In the meantime, in one of those freak examples of irony, it was announced that the four-year investigation into his share dealings by the Department of Trade and Industry had come to an end and he was completely exonerated. 'I always believed my name would be cleared,' said Piers. 'I may be unemployed, but I'm not a crook.'

Richard Wallace was named as the new editor of the *Mirror* – Piers really was Fleet Street history now. But you don't get to be the youngest newspaper editor for a generation without something to back it up and, while he was in this curious state of limbo, a few wheels started to turn. For a start, Piers began to write his memoirs; he had, after all, been at the centre of the action for many years and he might as well share his experiences. The deal was thought to be worth about £1 million, while it was reported that he received a further £1.7 million pay-off from the *Mirror*. (Piers later claimed it was much more than this.)

He began to gather himself together. Did he regret his anti-war campaign? 'Absolutely not! History will judge the *Mirror*'s campaign on the Iraq War as one of the strongest, bravest and best campaigns that any newspaper ever waged against anything ever and I believe that passionately,' he insisted, and, although the jury is still out, he may well have been right. 'When you look at it now, there is a very sound argument for putting him [Saddam] back – and how believable is that?' he continued. 'Armed fighters are swarming all over Iraq. We have devastated the region beyond any repair in the short term at all. None of this was going on while Saddam was in charge of things.'

And what of the pictures, did he regret publishing them? 'I regret it being the cause of my departure. I regret the fact that everyone thinks I was some naive idiot who was easily duped. I certainly resent that allegation, because a lot of people believed that they were genuine. The British Army believed they were genuine when they saw them, the Government believed they were genuine. I don't resent the fact that they let me go. I always wanted to go out with a bang anyway, and you certainly couldn't go out with a bigger bang than that – bigger than the Queen Mother – rather than falling sales and two paragraphs on page 23,' he insisted.

And, in October of that year, a part-time soldier – a private in the Territorial Army – appeared before a Court Martial, accused of perpetrating the hoax.

Piers' forthcoming memoir looked set to be a success. For more than a decade now, he had been at the centre of events and had met pretty much everyone, from show business to politics. 'I am not going to betray genuine confidences and I am not going to stitch people up who I don't think deserve stitching up, but lots of people have betrayed my confidences and lots of people have treated me pretty badly over the years – and I have no compunction at all in settling those scores in terms of revelation,' he said. 'It would be pompous to say it is historical, but it is certainly an interesting insight into what went on and how he [Tony Blair] changed, and Gordon Brown and the other cabinet ministers rose and changed.'

He was typically bullish about his time at the paper, too. 'Looking back on the *Mirror*, of the twenty biggest tabloid stories of the past decade, the *Mirror* probably had fifteen of them,' he told one interviewer. 'We carried on breaking huge stories, punching way above our weight journalistically, while unfortunately punching way below our weight financially.' He also recognised that his serious news agenda hadn't worked. 'I really thought that we were on to something – serious popular journalism – and it was some of the best popular journalism I was ever involved in,' he admitted. 'We won all the awards and everyone thought it was brilliant – apart from the readers. The masses decided it was too much for them and they turned away from it. It is a huge regret to me.'

And as for the anti-war stance: 'Eighty per cent of the British public were against the War before it started, yet, once it started and was on TV every day and became like this glorified, horrible video game, the patriotism kicked in. We had been just as critical of the Afghanistan War without any problem at all, so I was slightly emboldened by that and I didn't think we would have anything like the problem we had. Television was the difference.'

And so it was to prove in his own life. As he began to explore his next options, despite a long history of print journalism, he clearly began to realise that his future lay in television. Indeed, with hindsight, it almost looks as if he was preparing for a jump into another medium, although at the time he was just casting around for new projects. Gradually, it all began to take some kind of shape. In 2005, it was announced that he would be presenting *This Morning* while Phillip Schofield was on leave. A new life was slowly beginning to take shape, although this was never without its moments – once on *This Morning*, Piers inadvertently sparked fears of another terrorist attack, speculating about an atrocity in the run-up to the US presidential elections, while not realising that he was broadcasting live on air.

'I tell you what, I would brace yourselves for something in the next few days,' he told Fern Britton.

'Why?' asked Fern.

'I just think that al-Qaeda, with an election – I think they have been waiting for the election.'

At this point, the producers managed to let the presenters know their discussion was going out live on air.

'Good morning!' said Piers hastily. 'On today's show...' But he was cut off as time ran out.

A quarter of an hour later, *This Morning* actually began, with some embarrassment all round. 'I want to put everyone's minds at rest: we had a live television slip-up earlier where we usually do our promotion for the show and it goes out live, as a lot of you saw, and we didn't realise we were live,' admitted Fern. 'Don't panic, nothing is about to happen.'

'We were getting quite political and I was expressing that there had been a CIA report yesterday that was leaked, that they were worried about a terrorist attack in America before the US election,' added Piers. 'I don't know anything, so, if any of you are worried that I have any inside information about any terrorist attack, I don't. I hope that clears that up – we were just having a little private conversation. It's nothing new, there have been loads of rumours and speculation, but I'm sure nothing will happen.'

'That's something that you don't have to be a spy to understand, that possibly with an election coming up something may happen,' added Fern.

'Trust me, nobody tells me anything any more,' insisted Piers.

In November 2004, he teamed up with the journalist Amanda Platell to present a political talk show, in which he would represent left-wing politics (not necessarily his natural stance, despite his editorship of the *Mirror*), while she would judge proceedings from the right. It was meant to be serious television but the two never quite gelled, the show didn't exactly take off and it was judged a disappointment. It limped on for another two seasons, while failing to make a splash, but it made its mark on one person at least.

Over at the *Daily Telegraph*, the gossip column 'Spy' ran this item: 'After poor reviews of his Channel 4 debut with former Tory spin doctor Amanda Platell on Saturday, Spy hears that Piers Morgan already has another television project in the pipeline. I can reveal that the ex-*Mirror* editor is being lined up to present a prime-time debate and entertainment programme on BBC2 in the New Year.'

The editor of 'Spy' – and, indeed, the author of this item – was a journalist called Celia Walden. Nearly six years later, she would become Piers' second wife.

CHAPTER ELEVEN

THE INSIDER

In early 2005, Piers' first book of memoirs – *The Insider* – came out. It proved that, although he might no longer be sitting in the editor's chair, he was still capable of making the headlines; he had known everyone, been everywhere and wasn't afraid to name drop. And name drop, he did.

As for Cherie Blair, who he said disliked him: 'I don't hate Cherie. She had an extremely difficult upbringing that left her pretty damaged. She's not dissimilar to Diana in that respect. The last time I saw her was at Peter Mandelson's leaving do, where she flirted with me. The chivalrous thing is to say that I wouldn't be her type.' He followed up that statement by calling her 'breathtakingly capricious and vindictive, if not in the grip of a personality disorder'.

Blair himself, meanwhile, came across as a smidgen sycophantic in the book. They first met when Piers was editing the *News Of The World*. 'I want a good relationship with you and the *News Of The World*,' he had said. 'I don't want to get chewed up and spat out, like Neil Kinnock was by the *Sun*.' However, the two men, probably recognising in each other equally able operators, managed to get on.

Then there was Princess Diana, who gave Piers the story of how she suffered from bulimia and then, when the news came out, claimed outrage. 'Yep, she completely kippered me there,' he told one interviewer. 'I hope people read that and their jaws drop. My God, she was brilliant! I saw a lot of similarities between Cherie and Diana, who were both from damaged backgrounds. I loved Diana, she was intoxicating, but she was also difficult. She treated her domestic staff appallingly, was emotionally unstable and froze people out: Fergie, her mother, Elton John – terrible behaviour towards anyone who got too close.'

It seemed Piers was everywhere, even advising Prince William to get the powers that be to leave his late mother's butler, Paul Burrell, alone – Burrell was prosecuted for theft in 2002 and, after the charges were dropped, opened up like a geyser on the subject of Diana and has yet to pipe down.

He also revealed how lunch with Marion and Marco Pierre White resulted in a food bill of £260 and a wine bill of £26,000.

So whose diary would Piers most like to read? 'Mine,' he replied shamelessly. 'It's an absolutely riveting read – I've never enjoyed a book so much as when I read my own manuscript on holiday. What I've discovered is that my gut instinct that I was the most interesting person out there was right – that's a joke. As for other people's diaries, I'd quite like to read Boris Johnson's real diary.'

In the aftermath, Piers claimed that he hadn't really ruffled that many feathers and lots of the people featured in the book were still his friends. 'I had more complaints from people who wanted to be in who weren't than from those who were in,' he insisted. 'Given that there was a lot of score settling, I was surprised no one took me on, and disappointed, actually. Blair hinted in the *Evening Standard* 'Diary' that I'd exaggerated the number of times I'd seen him, but I took the meetings out of diaries prepared by my secretary. I saw him more than fifty-six times; those were the ones where it was me and him or me, him and a couple of *Mirror* journalists – I probably saw him one hundred and fifty times in all.'

Given how cavalier he was being about everyone else's private life, it was hardly surprising when one *Sunday Telegraph* reporter asked about his own. 'You can ask, but I won't tell you,' said Piers. 'If the *Sunday Telegraph* deems my private life to be in the public interest, they must pursue it aggressively, do an investigation. What you're not going to get is me helping you purely because it would make me squirm to talk about it. I can never understand why anyone would want to talk about their sex lives in print but some people do in *Hello!* (or wherever), perhaps I'm old-fashioned. Put it like this, I think it is wrong when politicians use their wives as a marketing tool: they use a photo of themselves with their wives to show they are a certain kind of man. I don't claim to be that sort of man – well, I haven't been with my wife for four years. That is not to say I do not believe journalists have a perfect right to scrutinise my life and come after me. Despite everything Ian Hislop says, I have never complained about it, not least because it would make me look a hypocritical twat.'

By now, his affair with Marina was over (not that Piers ever admitted publicly to the relationship), but he was about to meet the woman who would become the second Mrs Morgan. Meanwhile, in his public life, he was still casting about for something to do. The book had been a huge success, but it wasn't going to go on forever, and his television career wasn't really taking off. In May 2005, Piers took Fleet Street by surprise when he bought the newspaper trade's rag, the *Press Gazette*, in a deal worth between £500,000 and £1 million. His co-owner was the PR guru Matthew Freud, but this was a deal that would blow up in their faces.

Piers was now a proprietor – but of what? The *Press Gazette*, a forty-year-old weekly, had suffered badly in recent years. Once well respected, it had now run into problems as it had lost a good deal of its advertising, not least job adverts, which were now listed on internet sites. It was still doing well one night of the year, though, when it held the highly profitable British Press Awards, but that was to change, too.

Piers usually had pretty immaculate timing but, on this

occasion, it well and truly let him down. The previous British Press Awards had been held a couple of months earlier, but proved such a disaster that eleven national newspapers threatened to boycott the event in the following year. The whole affair descended into chaos when the *Sun* won an award for its Band Aid coverage; although the prizes were supposed to be secret, the paper's representatives just happened to have Bob Geldof in their midst, who made a long and very ill-advised speech, lashing out to all and sundry and making a fool of himself. There would always be drunkenness and brawling at these events (after all, this was where Jeremy Clarkson had punched Piers), but this year things got so bad that even the journalists were disgusted by it all.

Against this background (and the dinner was almost the only thing to turn a profit for the *Press Gazette* in those days), Piers and Matthew would have been better advised to set a match to their money and watch it burn instead. What's more, the deal only made things worse because of who they were: Piers had a lot of friends on Fleet Street, but he had made plenty of enemies too – especially on papers that he had dumped on as an editor. The success of his book and his general cockiness grated on some people, too. And so it was that a fair few newspapers decided they would not support either the dinner or the magazine, bringing it to the verge of collapse. (It now exists as a website, a shadow of its former self.)

Nor was anyone any happier about Matthew Freud's

presence at the table; he was one of the most successful PRs in London, but there is a fine line between journalism and public relations, and many journalists felt extremely uneasy that it had seemingly been crossed. To have their house journal, as it were, in the hands of someone who worked for a profession that some viewed as the enemy was too much; the deal never stood a chance.

Not that you would have guessed any of this, listening to Piers. He was cock-a-hoop about his purchase, determined it would expand to cover all sections of the media. Initially, it was not obvious how great the backlash would be – and not just from other newspapers either. Some readers even cancelled their subscriptions as a form of protest. Ray Hoppkrofft of Todmorden, West Yorkshire wrote, 'I wouldn't put money into the pocket of such a vile creature as Piers Morgan via the *Mirror* and I ain't gonna do so via the *Press Gazette*' – only for his correspondence to end up in the letters' column of the *Press Gazette*.

This was typical Piers. 'It's hilarious,' he said. 'I love that sort of stuff. I told them, "Fine, put it in."' And he was full of plans for his new future in the trade press. 'I went and bought all of them last week – *Campaign, Media Week, Marketing Week, Broadcast, Retail Week*. I saw lots of ideas that we can nick, shamelessly. People will think less of me if I didn't. I also saw a lot of crossover to interesting features we can do in *Press Gazette*. We are going to have more coverage of magazines, more coverage of PR, advertising, the internet.

'I want to have every single tentacle of Fleet Street covered. Every other part of the media will read *Press Gazette* to find out what's going on in the minds of journalists. I think, in terms of the basic emphasis of the magazine, it's going to be about the people that make the British media tick. I'm very interested in the people, not cold statistics or hard facts. I'm interested in the people that run the big media buying companies, that run the big PR agencies. These people are as interesting to journalists as the people who run papers, and we need to be very broad-thinking in that way.'

In an imaginative move, at this point, he hired the PR relations specialist Max Clifford as a columnist but it never really paid off.

Piers then announced that he would be going into the office at least once a week (as owner, his presence was not required quite so much). In truth, it looked more of a hobby than anything else. For all of the *Press Gazette*'s undoubted qualities, it was not a publication in the league he was used to dominating, and it was later estimated that in the course of his ownership – which lasted until the end of 2006, when the magazine went into administrative receivership and was sold off to a trade buyer – he actually only went into the office about six times. Here was a major media player casting about for his next big project and the *Press Gazette* was never going to be it.

Although it had yet to take a firm shape, his television work continued. Piers started to make documentaries on subjects ranging from social issues, such as hoodies, to the haunts of the wealthy albeit tacky, such as Marbella. He began a series of interviews for *GQ* magazine and landed a diary on the *Mail*; he also pursued his passions of cricket, football (Arsenal) and generally having a good time. Indeed, he now presented his exit from the *Mirror* as one of the best things that ever happened to him.

'We went to the Barbados test match last year and Ian Botham had been lent this 80ft racing yacht,' he told one interviewer. 'So, I'm lying on this fabulous yacht with Ian Botham, telling stories and thinking, life does not get better than this. So then I came back and got fired. I thought, great – I can do it more often!'

Nor, he said at the time, did it really knock him sideways (although later he was to admit this was an extremely difficult period). 'I waited a long time – I think my mother did, too – for the crash, but it never came,' he insisted. 'I found the whole thing very entertaining. Had a bit of a party the night it happened, went down to my village the next day and had another party – everyone seemed to find it terribly funny – and for a whole number of reasons it felt like the right time. I thought, if you're going to go, go with a huge bang. Much better than going out like a damp squib for poor sales.'

At this stage, it seemed as if he was champing at the bit to get back into newspapers. After all, he was still only forty – younger than when most people become editors – and talked slightly longingly about making a comeback as an editor when he was forty-five, but it was hard to know where that might be. The Mirror Group was out of the question and so too was News International, home of the *Sun* and the *News Of The World*. Nowhere else had any vacancies. Piers now found himself in the odd position of still being best known as a newspaper editor, but with nothing to edit. His proprietorship of the *Press Gazette* was not going well either, not least because the magazine was a dying force.

And then, another newspaper did come up, though admittedly nothing like any publication that he had edited before – indeed, nothing like it existed elsewhere. *First News*, a newspaper written by adults for children, was the brainchild of Nicky Cox (who had set up the children's magazines division at BBC Worldwide) and her cousin Sarah Jane Thomson (part of the media monitoring company Thomson Intermedia). The paper was to appear once a week on Fridays and would tackle serious news, as well as celebrity gossip, competitions and sport.

While it might not have been editorship of the *Mirror*, it was all good fun and a new challenge. Piers would be editorial director and he clearly looked forward to his new role. 'They needed somebody they thought would send a message that it was a serious operation as a newspaper,' he explained. 'I was very excited when I saw the dummies. I thought it was a great idea because there's a complete gap in the market for this, always has been. Clearly, it's uncharted waters but I wouldn't be wasting my time on something I didn't think would work. Nor would the Thomsons – everything they've touched in the world of media has gone platinum very quickly. They are putting millions into this and they have a long-term commitment to it.'

First News was to be aimed at nine- to twelve-year-olds, the age range of Piers' three sons. 'It will be sold alongside newspapers, not next to the *Beano*,' he proudly told one interviewer. 'There will be a round up of world events. We want it to be campaigning as well, particularly on kids' issues. A website (www.firstnews.co.uk) will run with it. The idea is for *First News* to become a forum for debate for that age group. We don't think anything is off limits. But it's not aimed at teenagers – there won't be "Position of the Week". We would definitely have splashed on Jamie Oliver's food campaign. It was a good political battle, relevant to children's lives, but we wouldn't have covered Tessa Jowell and David Mills because it's too complicated. I'm forty and I've edited newspapers, and *I* don't understand it. There has to be a limit on what you foist on young kids.'

However, he wasn't about to shirk away from the tough stuff either. 'My kids ask me questions about Iraq,' he continued. 'They see it on TV and they are not too sure what it's all about. We'll cover it with graphics – you have to make it exciting and easy on the eye. It won't be politically biased; it won't be right wing or left wing – it will be independent. So don't worry, the paper won't be full of all my old *Mirror* campaigns which I couldn't quite finish off.'

As with everything he did, debate began to rage about whether or not his latest venture would be a success and who would buy it, and if, as Piers said, it really was the first paper of its kind (in fact, there had been other children's newspapers in the past). 'It shows there's an appetite there,' he insisted. 'There are 193 magazines directly targeted at nine- to twelve-year-olds in this country and there has never been a proper newspaper. We think it's an untapped market. In France, the biggest-selling paper is a kids' paper and it sells 200,000 a day. No one has tried to do it properly in this country. I'm pretty confident we will do pretty big numbers; we are much more voracious buyers of newspapers than the French, so there has to be a chance we can accelerate to 200,000 to 300,000 copies. We don't want to set targets we can't hit, but we think there's a completely open marketplace.'

Whatever the outcome, his enthusiasm was infectious but there were other developments in the background, too.

For a start, although completely unknown to the wider public (not least because Piers refused to talk about his private life), he and Celia Walden were now an item. He was still not formally divorced, but his marriage to Marion was so firmly in the past that it was only a matter of time.

What's more, his television career was also going well. Of course, he had been appearing on television for years and had graduated to such senior roles as being a guest on both *Parkinson* and *Dame Edna Everage*, but he increasingly hosted shows himself. Rather naughtily, perhaps he was also making a documentary called *The Real Cherie*, but others (and they were increasingly focused on real-life stories) were on the lines of *You Can't Fire Me, I'm Famous*, talking to such celebrities as Martine McCutcheon, Donny Osmond, Ozzy Osbourne, Vinnie Jones and Naomi Campbell (now they were friends again) about what happened when life took a turn for the worse. Piers displayed a natural empathy for his subjects many wouldn't have credited him with. He also came across well on screen: a touch of arrogance, perhaps, but on the whole he seemed more self-confident than anything else. It might have taken him a while to get there but he was becoming a natural on TV.

Of course, the title of his new show was ironic, Piers himself having had an extremely high-profile sacking, and yet again it showed he had lost none of his instinct for what makes good copy. First on the show was Martine McCutcheon, who entertained enormously not only because she talked dramatically of being sacked from the role of Tiffany in *EastEnders*, but also in revealing that, when she filmed *Love Actually* with Hugh Grant, a friend dared her to put her tongue in his mouth in the kissing scene. She was all set to do so, she admitted, when he got there first!

Piers was simply brilliant at eliciting stories such as this and it was exactly how he had started out, first as a cub reporter and then on 'Bizarre' – getting the famous to admit to cheeky goings-on. But not every journalist in the print medium can transfer this skill to the small screen and he was getting better with every passing week. Ozzy Osbourne was next up, revealing that, when he bit off a bat's head on stage in the 1980s, he was promptly rushed to hospital to be tested for rabies. He then disclosed the reason why he stopped trying to kill his wife Sharon: 'After I was charged with murder, I've never touched her since.'

Naturally, all the guests were carefully selected; Piers might have been good at charming stories out of them, but he and his production team still picked pretty good subjects on whom to work their charm. If 'charm' is the right word, that is. Matters took a slight turn for the bizarre when Vinnie Jones came on to talk about the day he nearly bit the nose off a journalist, an act that resulted in his being fired as a newspaper sportswriter. The person who fired him, it turned out, was none other than one Piers Morgan, then editor of the *News Of The World*. Vinnie was so upset by the decision that he went into the woods behind his home intending to commit suicide, but didn't go ahead and instead went on to enjoy a highly successful acting career.

While the series might not have been making the front pages, it was still pretty good going – the shows were at least being talked about. In a more minor way, Piers was setting the agenda once again. Rather more significantly, he was beginning to make a name for himself in the US, for he had started to appear on *America's Got Talent*. The reason for this – and it was to be a crucial turning point in his new life – was that music executive and entrepreneur Simon Cowell had suggested him as a judge because he himself was unable to appear due to the conditions of his *American Idol* contract. In fact, this was to be a life-changing show for Piers.

David Hasselhoff, one of his fellow judges, summed up what was happening to him now. 'Piers! Piers is piercing,' he said. 'Piers is rude. All of America hates him because he made a little boy cry on the show, ha! But now that he is a star, I have taught him that he is fair game because of all the crap he used to write about us: welcome to our world, Piersy, pal! I am going to tell everyone that he is gay and see how he likes it.'

But Piers took it all in good part; asked what his guilty pleasure was, he replied, 'It would have to be David Hasselhoff. He is my fellow judge on an American show called *America's Got Talent*, where performers compete for a £1 million prize. It must be Hasselhoff, everything about him smacks of guilty pleasures.'

And there was a serious point behind all this: Piers was now becoming a mainstream celebrity. No longer a high-profile editor, rather he was growing famous in his own right, as much as the celebrities that he himself used to feature in his newspapers. If the *Press Gazette* wasn't going so well (and, by the end of 2006, both he and Freud appeared to have had enough), then he could afford to take it on the chin because he was beginning to move into a different league: he was on the verge of becoming an A-list star.

Certainly, his already high profile was coming along in leaps and bounds. He continued to pen profiles for *GQ* magazine and spread himself across the media in Britain, while in the US he unleashed a stream of vitriol towards contestants that had the country both thrilled and bemused. 'Are you deaf? Are you dumb? Or are you just so arrogant about that act that you think that's all you have to do?' he asked Quick Change, a magic duo. The female half left the stage in tears, while the male spat, 'You're allowed to judge, but you're not allowed to belittle.'

But this was something that Piers was good at and it increased his profile no end. He knew exactly what he was doing, too. 'The British public, quite rightly, thinks it's great fun to abuse, heckle and generally deflate the massively inflated egos of people who throw themselves on the altar of celebrity,' he wrote in one of his many media outlets. 'America is different. Fame there, in any degree, is a badge of honour and respect. Americans love celebrities: they revere them, salute them, want to touch them, bask in their reflected glory.' Piers, however, wasn't about to bask in anyone else's reflected glory and this went down a treat with the Americans.

Now on the verge of becoming a major star, he was doing so well in the US that there were plans afoot to run a similar programme on British TV. Even so, he refused to take anything for granted; leaving the *Mirror* in the way he did had been a shock, however much he might insist that he'd had it coming, and the new world of show business he'd so recently entered was one of the most insecure on the planet.

'The second series might flop,' he told an interviewer from the *Independent on Sunday*. '*Britain's Got Talent* might not get re-commissioned and I'll be back, talking to a bunch of bank clerks in Liverpool. That would be life. I sincerely want every *Independent on Sunday* reader to know I share their view that it would be much more fun if I fell flat on my face in about a year and a half's time.'

In fact, he was already faltering in one respect. In December 2006, the *Press Gazette* went into receivership, losing Piers about £250,000 (although, given the projects he was now working on, he could perhaps afford to take a loss). Eventually, it was rescued and given a new life on the internet where it remains to this day, but that chapter of his life was firmly closed.

Despite this setback, his personal life was much happier. He and Marion were still technically married, but the relationship with Celia was going from strength to strength. Marion herself, meanwhile, had a new boyfriend: the *News of the World* showbiz columnist, Rav Singh. It would be a while before the couple divorced but everyone involved had already calmed down about the separation.

At the beginning of 2007, Piers continued to make television appearances, signing up for a celebrity version of *The Apprentice* for Comic Relief. His fellow contestants were former No. 10 spin doctor Alastair Campbell, actor Ross Kemp, DJ Danny Baker, actor Rupert Everett, singer Cheryl Cole, comic Jo Brand, actress Maureen Lipman, style guru Trinny Woodall and Birmingham City football boss Karren Brady. It was all in a good cause and kept his profile high. The teams were boys versus girls and they were tasked with running a celebrity funfair on London's South Bank.

Cheryl Cole, also to make quite a name for herself on the back of reality TV, described the experience. 'It was much worse than the nerves I get before I go on stage because I was completely outside my comfort zone,' she admitted. 'When I walked in on the first day, I felt intimidated. I thought, what am I doing here with all these people; what the hell am I going to be expected to do? I knew it was important that we raised lots of money for Comic Relief so I felt a great sense of responsibility.'

There was a bit of a clash on the day, unsurprisingly involving Piers. A chef from the nearby restaurant Cecconi's went to help the girls; Piers attempted to capture him and ended up being kneed by Trinny Woodall. 'Trinny is a very dominant personality, very strong-minded,' said Cheryl. 'People think I am feisty but I seemed quiet by comparison. I was scared she might criticise my clothes, but luckily I escaped.

'She was a pretty impressive negotiator and managed to get a friend of hers to pay £150,000 for a ticket for our funfair. I was speechless: this woman offered the money like it was nothing – people buy a house for that amount. With the likes of Piers on the boys' team, I thought we would stand no chance so I just started ringing everyone I knew. The rest of the band came to help me. I was so grateful when the girls arrived that I threw my arms around them. [Her then husband] Ashley also came down to help. I got Simon Cowell and Chris Evans along too, so I was pretty pleased with myself. [But] there was bitching among the girls; it wasn't all smooth sailing.'

In fact, it made for extremely entertaining television. All the celebrities were called on to drum up contacts to make donations but it was Rupert Everett who froze. 'Julia Roberts, Sharon Stone, a genuine superstar of that ilk,' urged Piers. 'Tell Madonna to stop buying babies and chip in a bit.'

'I've been going through my address book – I don't know anybody,' Rupert rather tragically insisted. 'I have virtual relationships with people. You know what I mean?'

'Not really, no,' said Alastair Campbell, perhaps unhelpfully.

'I don't know any of these people particularly well,' continued Rupert, 'and I'm frozen in front of the camera.'

'But you're an actor,' countered Piers.

'Yes, but you need dialogue to be an actor. Anyone got a cigarette?' was Rupert's response.

'Please don't smoke,' said Alastair. 'I hate smoking.'

Everett subsequently walked out of the competition.

'We should demand another celebrity,' pronounced Piers, 'preferably one who doesn't answer to the description Big Girl's Blouse.' He then managed to persuade Anne Robinson, Chris Evans and Mick Hucknall to help out and personally raised about £200,000. The girls did really well, however, in getting Take That to man the dodgems. The girls' team won, and Alastair Campbell, leader of the losing boys' team, took Piers and Danny back into the boardroom again, where one of them would be fired. Campbell started off by having a go at Piers, telling him that he should know a lot of celebrities through his newspaper work and life in show business.

'I do!' insisted Piers.

'No, you *say* you do,' said Alastair.

'It's your demeanour that has cost you this,' decided Sir Alan Sugar. 'Piers Morgan, you're fired.'

'*Again?*' asked Alastair.

Off screen, Piers' first book had done so well that a second – *Don't You Know Who I Am?* – was subsequently commissioned and published in 2008. Again, a fuss was made as more indiscretions hit the streets. Of course, he himself was enjoying the whole experience for he had finally owned up: losing his job had been hard but it was beginning to come good. At last, his sacking was shown to be a tremendous piece of good luck, given that he was now firmly on the road to becoming extremely rich and famous.

CHAPTER TWELVE

BRITAIN'S GOT TALENT

Piers had been a huge success as a judge in *America's Got Talent*, although he was also a somewhat controversial figure. In the US version of the show, he was becoming known for the rigour of his opinions, but he was also being tough on small children. 'You are not as good as Beyoncé, you don't look like her and, frankly, your mother probably pushed you out there,' he told one six-year-old girl, provoking the wrath of none other than Jerry Springer.

'Stop it, that's wrong!' he told Piers live, before adding on the show's blog, 'I really was upset with Piers – I think that was out of line.'

Nor was it the end of the matter. 'First, you do not attack a six-year-old,' he told the magazine *TV Guide*. 'You also can't invite [kids] on the show and then attack them for coming; that is too much pressure.'

And it wasn't a one-off either; a nine-year-old called

Breeze had also come to Piers' attention. 'I feel it's not so much about you but what your mum wants,' he told her. 'She's pushed you into doing this and what she really wants is a million dollars and a new car.'

Springer (who knew something about making good television) brought the mother out to defend herself, but Piers was having none of it. 'I just don't believe a word of that,' he insisted.

It might have been unkind but it certainly got him noticed, as did the interviews he continued to do for *GQ*. Quite a few made the headlines, as when Boris Johnson, then Shadow Education Minister, confessed to drug-taking. 'I think I was once given cocaine, but I sneezed and so it did not go up my nose. In fact, I may have been doing icing sugar,' he recalled. 'There was a period before university when I had quite a few [joints], but, funnily enough, not much at university. It was jolly nice but apparently it is very different these days, much stronger. I have become very illiberal about it – I don't want my kids to take drugs.'

Piers then asked him if he could imagine having sex with Cherie Blair.

'I could, yeah. No, don't put that in! God! Not me,' was Boris's reply.

It was one of a series of colourful admissions that would provide the nation with great entertainment and kept Piers in the limelight as much as those he was interviewing.

But the real spotlight was now on *Britain's Got Talent*,

which started in June 2007. Following the success of the US version of the show, it was now considered ripe for a run in the UK. The series featured a succession of amateur entertainers, some very raw indeed, in front of three judges: Piers, Simon Cowell and actress Amanda Holden. It was to turn into one of the biggest success stories on television, but to begin with, of course, no one quite knew where it would go.

The show deliberately harked back to the days of seaside talent shows. 'Well, I've always been a big fan of entertainment in the 1950s and 1960s,' explained Cowell. 'To me, that was the absolute pinnacle. There was a kind of naivety in those days that I enjoy. We went through a phase in the 1990s when we became incredibly cynical and I didn't like that. Now we're back on track because I don't think tastes change.'

The whole team was very excited and Amanda Holden gave an interview about being approached by Cowell. 'Pretty much everything he touches turns to gold, so I was delighted to be asked,' she revealed. 'I sit between Simon and Piers Morgan, the former newspaper editor. Simon is always getting ribbed by Piers for draping his arm around my chair – he has a certain magnetic charm but that's just the way he is: he loves it. But both of them try to wind me up. If I say something they disagree with, they go, "What do you know, anyway?" But when I reply, "I've been in this business for fifteen years, I've auditioned, performed and acted, what do *you* know?" they soon shut up.'

And on screen Piers showed, crucially, that he could hold his own against Simon Cowell (not that anyone would have doubted it), while the two engaged in a friendly rivalry.

'Simon, you might be losing your touch,' Piers told him at one stage.

'I'm not,' said Simon. 'You're trying to make yourself popular – cheap!'

Amanda Holden summed it up. 'Simon and Piers are just like naughty schoolboys,' she said. 'They like to wind me up. If I disagree with their verdict, they say, "What do you know? You have no credibility." And I say, "So, Piers, weren't you sacked? And Simon, didn't you promote Zig and Zag?" That shuts them up! There is a real rivalry between them and they argue a lot on the show. I feel like their mother – like taking them by the scruff of the neck and saying, "Right, stop squabbling, it's straight to bed with no tea for you two."'

In fact, the chemistry between all three was working extremely well, although the reviews were mixed. 'The opening show saw Opportunity Knock for a bloke banging an ashtray with a set of keys (admittedly more talented than last year's X Factor runner-up, Ray Quinn), a kid who could make his ears squeak and Rupert "the piano-playing pig",' wrote the Mirror's television critic Jim Shelley. 'Even Cowell voted Rupert through. He and his sparring partner, TV's Piers Morgan, were in surprisingly charitable mood. (Come on, Piers! Call yourself American TV's new hate figure? I was relying on you to at least make some nasty remarks about Rupert having a long career ahead of him – as a round of bacon sandwiches.) He didn't do that badly, though. "Don't worry about him [Cowell] not liking you," Piers told the pig. "He likes to be the most talented pig in the room."'

Piers' reputation with children was still going strong, however, and he drew boos from the audience when he bluntly told child dancers Luke and Charlotte that he thought they'd be irritating but instead he had found them charming. Sometimes, he flirted with the contestants, as with Victoria Armstrong, a raunchy dancer from Manchester. 'I'd like to see more of you, Victoria,' said Piers. 'Literally.' He then asked her out for dinner.

Britain really was beginning to talk about the new series and the impact it was to have on the cultural life of the nation became ever more clear. As the final approached, the country became engrossed with an 'opera-singing phone salesman' garnering a lot of publicity; this was one Paul Potts, whose life was to change after his appearance on the programme.

'When I signed up to do this show, Simon Cowell and I shared a vision that there would be this guy doing an ordinary job, unassuming, who quietly had this amazing talent and that we could provide a platform so that the whole world could see what he could do,' pronounced Piers. 'You are that guy.'

And Simon Cowell agreed. 'This is what the show is all about,' he said. 'He's a normal guy, a great talent and came in as the underdog. It was one of the most incredible auditions I've ever seen. He can win if he can just repeat that performance. I wouldn't give him a makeover. Part of his appeal is that he's not trying. I could put him in Il Divo!'

All the best parts of *BGT* (and the various other projects Piers was involved in) featured a particular story that caught the public's imagination and in this case it was Potts. Paul (36 at the time and from Port Talbot) was a quiet and unassuming man, who had been working for the Carphone Warehouse when he appeared on the show. He had previously trained as an opera singer but, after he had had a benign tumour removed and then an accident in which he was knocked off his motorbike, he gave up singing for years until his wife Julie-Ann encouraged him on to the programme. When he first appeared, the audience giggled and the judges looked unsure – but then he opened his mouth and began to sing 'Nessun Dorma' and everyone was transfixed.

'I don't think they were expecting much,' Paul modestly said afterwards. 'I'm a bit short and overweight and had a cheap old suit on, and the hairdresser had used a No. 2 on my hair instead of a No. 4, so it made me look a bit bald. But, when I sang, I made sure I looked at the judges and saw Simon's jaw drop – I knew then I must have done all right.'

In fact, he ended up not only winning the series but also singing before HM the Queen at the Royal Variety

Performance. Headlines such as PAVA-POTTY appeared and the nation was enthralled.

Meanwhile, Kelvin MacKenzie watched his former protégé approvingly from the side. 'Congratulations to my friend Piers Morgan on doing something first achieved by The Beatles in the 60s – being No. 1 in America and Britain,' he wrote in his *Sun* column. 'Incredibly the show *Britain's Got Talent* and its American version are going out simultaneously this week, with Piers as a judge in both. The show is already number one in the US and, having seen the overnight ratings in which they thrashed *Big Brother* three to one, it's clearly number one over here. An astonishing achievement.'

Piers freely admitted that he had always loved celebrity and was enjoying his new life. 'It is something I always wanted since I was a showbiz editor in my early days as a journalist,' he declared. 'You don't get to meet the stars of stage, screen and music without something of their lifestyle drawing you to it like a magnet. It's a different world from what most of us are used to: the private jets, the yachts, the villas and the glamour. And it is a world of glamour. Of course, I wanted to be a part of it – most showbiz journalists feel like that.'

And now he truly was a part of it all. *Britain's Got Talent* proved a massive success, on top of which Piers was also becoming famous in the US. Another series of *You Can't Fire Me, I'm Famous* loomed, and he was his usual self-deprecating self on the subject. 'They agreed to do it with me because they know that I was also publicly humiliated about my sacking in the media,' he explained. 'We have something in common and the original interviews with people like Jade Goody, who cried for ages, Louis Walsh and Anne Robinson took three hours before being edited to the viewing length. Even Naomi Campbell agreed to be interviewed.'

So how was it, he was asked, when he himself became news in the wake of his own sacking? 'Awful. But it's what the press does – I should know that,' he responded. 'When it happened, it was quite devastating but it wasn't a case of finding out who my enemies were – I already knew the answer to that: it was who my friends were. They came to me, took me out for a Chinese or a beer, and it's nice to know that there are people like that who you rely on.'

He was certainly having the last laugh now. And, no matter how competitive they might have been on stage, he was well aware who he had to thank for his career renaissance: Simon Cowell. Indeed, Cowell was playing as important a role in Piers' career in his forties as Kelvin MacKenzie had done in his twenties and he wasn't about to forget it. 'I have been surprised at how things have accelerated in my career,' conceded Piers, 'but I owe everything to Simon Cowell. It was he who got me on to the *Britain's Got Talent* show and the American one. And both series were top-rated. I'm loving every minute of it, although Cowell can be a notorious prankster. When I walk on stage, he'll have arranged for the audience to call out or hold up placards saying: "Who are you?" Or he'll prime them to sit in total silence when I appear, then give me the slow hand clap.'

And he was absolutely loving his time in the spotlight. 'It really annoys me when certain celebrities moan about their star status and the attention they get,' he went on. 'People like Ian Hislop, who loves to dish it out to people but can't take it himself, or the luvvies of the acting world like Hugh Grant and Jude Law, who are forever saying they can't stand being photographed by the paparazzi everywhere they go and then purposefully go to places where the paparazzi will be.

'I certainly couldn't be like that. I love the attention, make no mistake about it, but, contrary to what people might think, I am not motivated by money. I don't want the huge houses and yachts – I've got a beautiful flat in London and a home in the country; I can take holidays at my favourite place in France, which is Eze, near Monaco, and that suits me fine.'

Indeed, everything in his life appeared to be going well, including family. Still officially married to Marion, he saw his children regularly and they were enjoying their father's stardom, too. 'My kids go to a weekly boarding school, the same as I did,' he said. 'They love it, because they come home every weekend and they are coming out to Los Angeles along with their mother soon, which is going to be marvellous because obviously I miss them, despite how concentrated I have to be on all of the work.'

You Can't Fire Me, I'm Famous continued to make headlines, too. In 2007, the late Jade Goody appeared in her first interview since the race row with Shilpa Shetty in the *Big Brother* house and before she was diagnosed with the cancer that was to kill her. The programme got a lot of attention. 'I had bad depression,' she told Piers when speaking about the aftermath of the *Big Brother* furore. 'I was on sleeping pills and on suicide watch. It's the worst thing a mother can say, "There's no hope." But I snapped out of that quickly because I've got kids and they are my life. I'm not doing this to be back in magazines or on TV, but I've got a mortgage and bills to be paid.'

And still there were those *GQ* interviews, too. In the latest, Sir Richard Branson admitted in fairly graphic detail to being a member of the Mile High Club. 'I was sitting in Economy on a Freddie Laker flight next to this very attractive lady as we headed to LA,' he recalled. 'We got chatting and it went a bit further. And it was every man's dream, to be honest. I was about nineteen, I think. I remember getting off the plane and she turned to me and said, "Look, it's slightly embarrassing but I am meeting my husband at Arrivals, would you mind holding back a bit?" But it was a memorable flight. The problem with plane loos generally is that they are very small and the acrobatics can't take too long because there's no room and people start banging on the door. What I remember vividly is seeing four handprints on the mirror as we finished and thinking I'd better wipe them off.'

This was followed by Anne Robinson on *You Can't Fire Me, I'm Famous* discussing her alcoholism. 'At the very end of my drink problem, around 1977, I weighed about six stone,' she confessed. 'The doctors gave me six weeks to live. I'd just stopped feeling – I lived in a haze and couldn't quite understand how it happened to me. But I couldn't stop drinking.' She finally managed to do so in 1978, and has remained dry ever since.

Around this time, everything Piers did made headlines and this included his sojourn in the States, as well. One of his fellow judges on *America's Got Talent* was the *Baywatch* actor David Hasselhoff, who took umbrage at something Piers had written about him in his book. He got his revenge, too; after Piers buzzed off a country singer called Jason Pritchett, the Hoff mused, 'It must be so hard to come out here and have some wanker buzz you off.' Stunned silence ensued.

Backstage, the Hoff remained unrepentant. 'I usually love Brits,' he said. 'After the US and Germany, I see the UK as my third home. They've always been supportive of everything I've done – but Piers? Well, he just takes things too far. He wrote something about me crying like a baby when I cut a nerve in my wrist. That was just not true – I was just so happy to still have my hand! I mean, I'm a single guy – I need the use of my hands, if you know what I mean! Seriously, he has crossed the line sometimes. Piers will say, "It's British humour." I don't mind someone joking about me, my music, whatever – but don't bring my kids or my family into it. He wrote some things in his book and he thinks it's acceptable. Well, I say that calling him a wanker on TV is acceptable, too!'

Meanwhile, Piers laughed it off. He was pretty good about laughing at himself, which was just as well, not least in August 2007 when he was pictured falling off a Segway. In no time at all, an old copy of the *Mirror* – then edited by him – came to light, with a picture of President Bush falling off a Segway: YOU'D HAVE TO BE AN IDIOT TO FALL OFF, WOULDN'T YOU, MR PRESIDENT? ran the headline. When Piers tried it, he broke two ribs, although that certainly didn't keep him away from the TV screens. Far from it: ebullient as ever, he was about to become even more high profile.

CHAPTER THIRTEEN
MASTER OF ALL TRADES

By the beginning of 2008, Piers' profile was becoming almost as high in America as it was in the UK. He took part in the US version of *Celebrity Apprentice*, presided over by Donald Trump, and won this time, triumphing over thirteen fellow contestants. 'You're a vicious guy; I've seen it. You're tough, you're smart; you're probably brilliant, I'm not sure. You're certainly not diplomatic, but you did an amazing job and you beat the hell out of everybody,' was how Trump congratulated him.

'It's a great day for evil, obnoxious, arrogant Brits everywhere,' Piers observed afterwards to the American radio station KIIS-FM on Friday. 'It's like a Simon Cowell production factory in Britain, where they create these utterly obnoxious people and we ship them over to America and you seem to lap it up.'

His tendency to sound off, however, especially when there were children around, was beginning to land him in trouble. In January 2008, there was an altercation at a *BGT* audition when Piers told one young boy that he wouldn't get through because there were 'plenty of dancers like you already'. The boy's father took exception, telling Piers, 'If you can't stand the heat, get out of the kitchen.'

Piers responded coolly, 'If you don't like criticism, don't let your son enter contests like this!'

This resulted in the man threatening him. 'If you ever speak to my son like that again, I'll come after you,' he raged.

Afterwards, Simon loaned Piers his bodyguard Tony until matters calmed down.

Super-busy as ever, Piers was asked to describe his job. 'I don't have just one any more, I have loads,' he explained, 'which means I can never get fired again because I can always claim that whatever I'm getting fired from is not my real job, just a hobby. This year alone, I'll be judging *Britain's Got Talent* and *America's Got Talent*, presenting an eight-part BBC1 interview series on fame, doing various other projects for ITV, writing my weekly column for *The Mail on Sunday*'s *Live* magazine, monthly interviews for *GQ* and my third volume of diaries, continuing to be editorial director of *First News* (the national newspaper for children that is starting to do incredibly well), making speeches everywhere from Dover to Dubai – and generally whoring myself as usual around the nation's airwaves. It's all vaguely ridiculous, but I love it.

'I like to think I act as a constant reminder of what

can happen if you resolutely refuse to take yourself as seriously as others wish to take you. The British media is full of hypocritical, pompous, booze-sodden, whining, cynical bores – and other people who just want to have a laugh before they die. I prefer hanging out with the second crowd and tormenting the first.'

What's more, he was being handsomely remunerated for his efforts. Being Piers, he couldn't help but boast about it, as when he was asked how much he earned. 'I don't want to reveal too much as I'm going through a divorce, but it's a good six figures – several multiples of the Prime Minister's salary,' he declared. 'It's far too much when you consider that most of the time I am sitting in a large leather chair in Hollywood, judging dancing horses and Mongolian contortionists. I earn money in a variety of ways these days – TV, books, magazine columns and interviews, newspaper articles, speeches and other commercial stuff. It all adds up to a fairly repulsive sum but then I pay a fairly repulsive tax bill, too.'

In fact, this was, if anything, understating the case, for it is estimated that Piers earned £4–£5 million in the first few years after being sacked. He was fast becoming an extremely wealthy man, with a fortune estimated at about £15 million.

Up until now, he had divided his time between a penthouse riverside flat in Fulham, where he moved after his marriage broke up, and a place in Sussex, near where he grew up, but he was finally getting divorced, not least because the relationship with Celia Walden was now serious, and he had to start thinking about somewhere else to live. And so he came up with an ingenious solution; it had been widely reported that Celia's father, former Tory MP George Walden, was none too keen on his daughter's beau, but his stance must have softened because Piers was to buy George's house. The Grade II-listed mansion in upmarket Kensington, West London, cost £4 million, a figure that Piers could now well afford, which must have endeared him to the man who was about to become his father-in-law. And, although he and Celia did not become engaged until the divorce had gone through, it was no secret that an engagement was now on the cards.

'Something like that is never going to make you feel good about yourself,' he told one interviewer about the break-up of his marriage. 'It's not an episode that made me feel great but it was a long time ago and I'm glad we managed to stay friends. We've got three great boys and they're growing up really well and it's all worked out fine. My wife's been really good about it all – always has been, and I respect her for that. She could have done things very differently, but she didn't. We've stayed friends and that's been incredibly important to me.'

He was typically irrepressible, though. When asked what had been his best investment in life, his reply was: 'Buying Simon Cowell dinner at Cipriani about three years ago. He had Spaghetti Bolognese, I had the veal and it cost me about £126. It ultimately landed me lucrative judging roles on *Britain's Got Talent* and *America's Got Talent*.'

And the worst? 'The day I decided to purchase shares in Viglen will probably go down as the least well-advised business decision made by a journalist. I sold all the shares and gave the proceeds to charity. I also lost about £250,000 on *Press Gazette*, the trade publication I bought with Matthew Freud in 2005; we revitalised the magazine and transformed the British Press Awards into a great event again. The only problem was that many of my old Fleet Street mates decided to knife us squarely in the back, for which I will be eternally ungrateful.'

Piers was now doing lots of other television work, too; he presented documentaries about people and places, including the millionaire's favourite in Dorset: Sandbanks. Meanwhile, his *GQ* interviews continued to set the agenda; there was widespread hilarity after he interviewed Nick Clegg, the Leader of the Liberal Democrats, in April 2008. Clegg was asked how many lovers he'd had. 'How many are we talking – ten, twenty, thirty?' asked Piers.

'No more than thirty – it's a lot less than that,' replied Clegg. 'I don't think I am particularly brilliant [as a lover] or particularly bad.'

So are reputations destroyed in an instant: Clegg became a national laughing stock and was branded 'Cleggover' by the political hacks, while Piers himself expressed surprise that the Lib Dem Leader had even answered the question. He would have been perfectly within his rights to say a gentleman didn't talk about such matters – but then Piers displayed a near genius in catching people off-guard. It was not until a full two years later, when Clegg put in a far more impressive performance in the run-up to the General Election than had been expected of him, that he regained his status as a serious politician. Piers, meanwhile, was frequently asked the same question in interviews from then on and routinely told his interviewers that he had no intention whatsoever of being drawn on the matter.

The editor of *GQ*, Dylan Jones, was pretty pleased with his star interviewer, too. He'd hired Piers 'on a whim' but even he had no idea how well the decision was going to turn out. 'The features team thought I'd gone mad. They said no one will want to have anything to do with him, [but] Piers is one of those journalists who can tap you on the arm and ask, "You did, didn't you? Come on, you can tell me." And he gets away with it.'

And Piers certainly elicited some startling revelations, as in the time actress Billie Piper admitted to lesbian sex fantasies and said she liked 'dirty straight porn'.

But the life of an international celebrity entails constant attention and Piers was now coming under constant scrutiny, too. He was not an exceptionally vain man, but he was spending a lot of time in Hollywood, the land of the perfect people, and beginning to worry about his appearance. Although he point-blank denies Botox (unlike the extremely image-conscious Cowell), he started working out with a personal trainer and also had his teeth whitened.

'I had my teeth whitened in Beverly Hills,' he revealed. 'It's my one and only failure to resist vanity. I got so fed up doing interviews in America, where they were banging on about how awful my teeth were, that I paid £300 to have it done. What no one tells you, though, is how painful it is. You get them done, they're bright white and you think, fantastic! And then the pain sets in. I'm actually a stone lighter than when I was editing the *Mirror*. I don't get hurt when people go on about the way I look; all I care about is what they say about my integrity. When I got fired from the *Mirror* for those Iraq photos, some people said I knew they were fakes; that cut me to the quick. My own brother was fighting in Basra the day I published those pictures and the idea I would put his life (and the life of those boys fighting with him) in danger is pretty damn unpalatable. That aside, the fact I'm a critic means I can't complain when people dish it out to me. And, if enough people say I look like a grotesque lump of lard, the upside is that when they meet me they'll say, "Oh, you're a lot slimmer than I thought you'd be."'

Celia, fortunately, was a very striking woman who could more than hold her own in the environment in which the couple now lived.

Paul Potts, incidentally, also had his teeth sorted out, something Piers commented on when he went to interview him for the *Sun*.

The next series of *BGT* began, prompting a great deal of attention and, at the same time, Piers started another interview series: *The Dark Side of Fame with Piers Morgan*. He was now becoming so famous as an interviewer as well as a judge on reality TV that it was a selling point to have his name in the title of the show. Guests were to include Mickey Rourke, Tracey Emin and Nancy Dell'Olio. He remained coy about it, though, saying he had no plans to sit in the chair vacated by Michael Parkinson.

'But I don't want to be the next Parky,' he insisted. 'He's a living legend, as is David Frost, and, if I could get anywhere near their standard, I'd die a happy man. But I've spent twenty years building up to this and, yes, I want the big chat show because I love meeting famous, iconic people, but I don't want to be the next Parky – I want to do it my way.'

He was about to get his wish. Meanwhile, he had not forgotten who was responsible for much of his success: Simon Cowell. 'Yes, it is weird and uncomfortable that Mr Cowell is in control of my destiny,' he admitted in one interview. 'In fact, when the show hit No. 1 here and in America he texted me, saying, "I feel like Dr Frankenstein – I've unleashed a monster." Even now, he still signs himself "Dr Frank" when he texts. But, seriously, I owe him a lot. It makes me cross when people constantly snipe at him. He works like crazy and he's totally loyal to his staff. Simon's one of the good guys, which is ironic, given his status as "Mr Nasty". However, he was an absolute bastard when he asked me to meet NBC bosses about *America's Got Talent*. No one knew who the hell I was, but he stuck his neck out for me and flew me to LA. I thought the meetings had gone pretty well but a few days later he rang and said in a really low voice, "Piers, it's not good news." I was crushed because I knew this could have been a huge break for me. He went on, "I've done everything I can but they're adamant, I'm afraid..." then there was a huge pause, "... that you're coming to Hollywood." I just screamed my head off and ran into the street, beating my chest like Tarzan.'

A sign of quite how far he'd come emerged at a charity auction for Leukaemia Research in May 2008. One of the lots was a day editing the *Mirror*, and Piers and the current *Mirror* editor, Richard Wallace, both made bids. In the event, Piers won after coughing up £12,000. Later, he said that he'd been drunk, which is why he put in a bid, but it was a pretty good way of demonstrating that he was now in a different league.

Indeed, although he tried not to talk about money, it was widely reported that, when he signed a deal with ITV in mid-2008, it was worth £2 million, a figure that was never denied. And these sorts of opportunities would continue with *BGT*, fronting documentaries and all kinds of interviews.

Over at *GQ*, another Lib Dem MP, Lembit Opik, was offering himself up; he was at the time engaged to Cheeky Girl Gabriela. How did she challenge him intellectually? asked Piers.

'One evening, we discussed the concept of a perfect circle, as a geometrical challenge,' Lembit replied.

Piers was loving his new life. 'Personally, I've been struggling to find my own dark side of fame,' he said in one interview. 'My skin is so thick, I suspect that if they tried to operate on me they wouldn't have a scalpel big enough: fame is a delightful mistress and I have no desire to return to anonymity whatsoever, trust me.' It seemed unlikely he would have to do so.

One interviewer flew out to LA to see what his life was like over there. Piers picked her up in an Aston Martin and he was off immediately. 'Firstly, well, you've got to have a nice car to be taken seriously in this town,' he told her. 'You've got to have at least an Aston Martin and then you get treated well by the valet boys, and that's half the battle. They can ignore you for days in a valet park – you can be left there from Monday to Friday. Literally. Secondly, you fly from Heathrow to LAX, first class, BA, and you get seat 1K. 1K's great, because your eye line naturally goes this way, which means other people can't see you, or they can see you but you can't see them seeing you. Show-offs sit in 1A, because they want to see themselves being seen. I didn't [get it] once, got 2K – I was spitting blood – but then I realised Michael Caine had got it, so that was OK. I sat behind him and Shakira, and they were very sweet. He called her "Sha" and he was talking exactly like, "Not a lot of people know that" – really enjoying going through the magazines, going, "Here, Sha, look at this car in this advert! Here, Sha, have you read this article?" Sweet. They're clearly madly in love – you could tell she just gets him.'

Like the mega-celeb he now was, Piers had groupies chasing him, too. '*Yes*, the best one I got was when I won the 2008 *Celebrity Apprentice*,' he recalled. 'At the party afterwards, I was talking to my mum and my sister – they'd flown out for it – and a very attractive blonde came up to me and touched my hand, dropped a piece of paper into it: she'd written her phone number on it. And she said, "Give me a call later, we'll hook up. And trust me, I'm no apprentice!" And my mother went, "Did she just do what I think she did?" I said, "I'm afraid so, Mother. They're called 'groupies'." I loved the moment – and she was bloody hot, too! But then to walk over to the bin and go, kacha!'

That kind of attitude makes it hard not to like Piers. In the past, he might have been a world-class feuder but now he was simply revelling in his new life, enjoying it, getting on with everyone, while admitting to being arrogant and pompous before anyone else could accuse him of it. He was shameless, but in a somehow likeable way. 'That is the benefit of becoming famous in your forties,' he said. 'You see the funny side of it, the absurdity. You find it endlessly entertaining, you don't take it seriously; you know there's a real world out there. And you know, however bad things get, there are people on sink estates in Glasgow, watching you on TV, dreaming that one day they'll have the glamorous life you are lucky enough to enjoy and you know they'll never experience it. You've got to remind yourself of that every single time you go on

TV: how lucky you are. I can't stand whingeing celebrities who whine about paparazzi and intrusion, and the hell of being famous.'

But he could be serious when necessary, too. Reality-TV star Chantelle Houghton, who'd shot to fame as the only non-celeb in *Celebrity Big Brother* a couple of years earlier, appeared on *The Dark Side of Fame* and talked about her disastrous marriage to the pop singer Preston. 'A month after we were married, Preston told me, "I knew I didn't want to marry you on our wedding day." It was weird on the day,' she said. 'He was pulling silly faces when we took our vows; he took the pee. I tried to keep a straight face but I thought he was being weird. I thought, you shouldn't be doing this, you should be looking into each other's eyes on your wedding day. I wondered what was going on, but I just went along with it. After he told me that he never wanted to marry me, we did interviews where we told everyone how happy we were. I lied about being happy.'

'I am shocked,' declared Piers. 'This is every bride's nightmare, being told your husband never wanted to marry you in the first place.'

And he meant it, too. Piers had developed empathy – and it was taking him all the way to the very top.

CHAPTER FOURTEEN

THE RHINO IN RIOT GEAR

At the start of 2009, Piers and *Britain's Got Talent* were in the news again, although this time it was because of the machinations of Simon Cowell. Much excitement was generated when it was announced that the curvaceous model Kelly Brook was to join the show as a fourth judge and rival to Amanda Holden; even more excitement ensued shortly afterwards when she was dropped. Rumours abounded as to what had gone wrong (possible reasons cited were that Kelly's performance was said to be wooden, the balance of the judges didn't work as well and she'd upset hosts Ant and Dec), but it was welcome publicity for a show that was about to produce a singing sensation to rival Paul Potts.

'It was very confusing for both us and the talent on the show,' Piers admitted afterwards. 'When there are four of you and two people vote one way and two vote the other, it gets difficult to decide who goes through.'

Everyone's feathers had got a little ruffled, it seemed, and the new signing certainly hadn't worked. 'Piers and Amanda are very close and weren't exactly welcoming to Kelly, though they were always professional on camera,' revealed an insider on the show, 'but, when the cameras stopped, she was the target of quite a few jokey asides from Piers, which had an edge to them. It was clear Amanda wasn't happy at having her role as the show's Queen Bee threatened. Most shocking of all was the fact that Ant and Dec were obviously unhappy – they are as big stars as Simon and felt snubbed when changes were made without telling them. Kelly was isolated: it's not easy working with people who barely mask their contempt and make your life hell.'

Meanwhile, Kelly herself was said to be very upset by Simon Cowell. Whatever the reality, the signing had clearly been a mistake for all involved.

At the same time, Piers' other television work was continuing with documentaries on Dubai and the Brits in Hollywood, as well as a series called *Life Stories*, which was another interview format and made for compelling viewing. It featured Swedish-born TV presenter Ulrika Jonsson talking about the time she was raped. 'I just lay there,' she recalled. 'And he said, "We should go to the cinema," and I said, "I can't go." I stayed and he left.'

By now, public opinion on Piers was divided quite sharply. People either liked or loathed him, something he was well aware of – and he even admitted that he wasn't quite the rhino in riot gear some folk made him out to be. He too had feelings, which could be hurt. 'People do actually come up in the street and say they really like me, but I know there are others who don't. I'm a bit like Marmite,' he told an interviewer on his old paper, the *Mirror*. 'My family don't recognise me on television. They say, "Why don't you just be yourself?" And I tell them it's because a lot of people know that I'm simply playing a role, plus it's quite lucrative. My mother goes to parties and there's always one or two who just want to hurl abuse at her about me. My youngest brother doesn't even admit to knowing me and I don't blame him – I wouldn't, either.

'Look, I used to clear the front page to bury people so I can't complain when it happens to me. I'm putting myself up to be whacked – it's part of the game – but does anyone like waking up and being called a fat, talentless, useless git? Not really. You pretend you don't mind, but underneath it all you want to kill the bastards. I take a huge deep breath, let it out and it just fades away. It takes ten seconds, then it's gone.'

Despite this, Piers was well and truly having the last laugh. Rich, famous and successful, with a happy relationship bubbling away in the background, he was fast reaching the stage where he had nothing else to prove but that did not stop him from taking a pop at Jonathan Ross, who at the time still had his chat show. Piers was rapidly becoming his closest rival and, according to him, it was because he marked a return to interviewing basics.

Meanwhile, Ross had recently become embroiled in a row over offensive messages left on the answering machine of actor Andrew Sachs and was widely believed to be living on borrowed time.

'What has happened to the chat show over the past ten years is that it has morphed into an entertainment vehicle for comedians and smart-Alec presenters, who mickey-take their guests for seven or eight minutes, plug some ghastly album, then get them off,' Piers explained. 'I just thought there was a gap in the market for what I call good old-fashioned chat, in which you forensically go over someone else's life. There are no conditions or stipulations for my six guests [on *Life Stories*]. None. I think what's interesting about Ross is that it started high with the comeback show because people were curious and it's now drifted about 300,000 or 400,000 below the average [ratings] for the series.

'I think it's got problems. It's just got very boring because he can't be the Jonathan Ross that got him where he was. He can't be lewd and offensive like he used to be, and he's ended up being a quite smarmy and sycophantic interviewer. I don't think he's worth the money and he should have been fired. I don't think any other broadcaster on British television – working for the BBC, where your salary is paid by the taxpayer – could have done what he did to Andrew Sachs and get away with it.'

And Piers was true to his word: his shows were compulsive viewing. The latest featured Richard Branson talking about the time when he was nearly expelled from school, aged thirteen, when he was caught sneaking out of the headmaster's daughter's bedroom. Piers' easy-going manner was indeed extracting one confession after another from his subjects – but without malice, too. There was none of the Ross-style attempt to make fun of the guests, just easy-going chat as Piers himself had promised.

Katie Price was next up, castigating herself for sleeping with Gareth Gates when she was pregnant and talking about the time when, as a child, she'd been approached by a paedophile in the park.

All this paled into insignificance, however, compared to what was to become one of the biggest stories of 2009, courtesy of *BGT*. For some time, rumours had been doing the rounds that there had been a remarkable discovery of an extremely gifted singer from a small town in Scotland but, until that particular episode was broadcast in April that year, the exact nature of the mystery artist had been a mystery. Now, both judges and audience watched, bemused, as a dumpy woman with an awful hairstyle and a frumpy dress came out on stage: her name was Susan Boyle. She told the crowd that she wanted to sing like Elaine Paige, which received a rather negative response. After this, she did some awkward gyrations and everyone was braced for certain embarrassment until she began to sing.

Susan Boyle's transformation from dowdy spinster to international star was truly a Cinderella story, with Piers and his fellow judges playing the role of Fairy Godmother. 'I am giving you the biggest "yes" I have ever given anybody,' Piers told her. 'You said you wanted to be like Elaine Paige and everyone laughed at you – you proved them wrong.'

Susan was a mass of contradictions: the voice of an angel, but the demeanour of exactly what she was, namely a forty-eight-year-old with learning difficulties who had never had a relationship. After that first appearance, she was rushed off to the hairdressers and grooming specialists, where she was generally smartened up and it appeared that she had developed a massive crush on Piers.

'Up until now I have never met the right man, but maybe that will change now I have met Piers,' she admitted after the show. 'He's a very handsome man. It is quite hard to choose between Piers and Simon because they're both lovely but I think it would definitely be Piers.'

And Piers responded with remarkable good humour. As media interest in Susan Boyle rocketed, he became a sort of protector for her. Behind the scenes were reports of eccentric behaviour and her family began to interfere in the whole process, calling on Simon Cowell to forget about putting her into the finals and get her signed up for a recording contract straight away. Piers was always there to calm things down, tell everyone that Susan was fine and was coping with the pressure; that everything would be all right. From his former role as troublemaker, he was now turning out to be the one bringing peace. And, as for Susan's increasingly ardent proclamations about how attractive he was, he never once allowed her on his behalf to become a figure of fun.

Indeed, both were interviewed on the American talk show *Larry King Live* – which Piers was about to take over – and he used the opportunity to charm her. 'The great appeal and charm of Susan is the way she is: she is her own woman,' he declared, before adding, 'I would like to extend an invitation to you to have dinner with me in London, Susan.'

'I accept,' said Susan.

Piers also apologised for the judges' reaction when she first came out on stage. 'We thought you were going to be a bit of a joke act, to be honest with you,' he admitted. 'I had never heard a more surprising, extraordinary voice coming out of somebody so unexpected.'

And the faux flirtation continued. In the semi-final of *BGT*, Susan sang 'Memory' from Andrew Lloyd Webber's musical *Cats* – 'This is for you, Piersy baby,' she cried.

Piers later recounted what happened after the show, 'I'm never going to forget what happened to me at 10.32pm last night,' he said. 'That was the moment when Susan Boyle ran down a flight of stairs at the Fountain Studios in North London, flung herself into my arms and planted a five-second "smacker" right bang on my lips!'

All his Hollywood chums, including Bruce Willis and The Hoff, expressed interest in this new phenomenon. But, as further reports of odd behaviour emerged, Piers became increasingly protective. 'Susan is finding it very, very difficult to cope and to stay calm,' he announced. 'She has been in tears many times over the last few days and even, fleetingly, felt like quitting the show altogether at one point and fleeing all the attention.' Yet still, she somehow managed to carry on.

In the event, Susan was pipped to the post by the all-male dance troupe Diversity, who won the show, but it was clear that a new star had been born. However, briefly, it seemed as if a crisis was at hand; clearly overcome by all the emotion and stress, Susan ended up staying at The Priory for a short spell of rehab, a move which led to widespread criticism of the way she'd been handled by the *BGT* team, and which Simon Cowell himself admitted could have been improved on. But the problem proved short-lived and she quickly became a star. At the time of writing, it is estimated that Susan Boyle has amassed a multi-million-pound fortune and she remains probably the biggest star ever produced from reality television.

Piers himself wasn't doing too badly, either. ITV was so pleased by the success of *Life Stories* that it moved the show to a primetime position on Saturday night – the slot once occupied by Michael Parkinson – to start in the autumn. Quite clearly, Piers was shaping up to be the prime interviewer of his generation. Affirmation of his status, if it were needed, came when he was invited on to another famous interview slot, although this time as a guest, when he appeared on Radio 4's *Desert Island*

Discs. His favourite record was 'Mambo Italiano' by Dean Martin, Brian Keenan's *An Evil Cradling* was the book he would like to take with him and his luxury was a cricket bat. There was also the most obvious hint to date as to just how serious his relationship with Celia Walden was becoming, 'I met Stevie Wonder last summer in LA,' he told presenter Kirsty Young. 'I got him to record on video a marriage proposal to Celia – so, should I ever need to use it, I have Stevie Wonder ordering Celia to marry me.'

That proposal, however, was still to come. In the meantime, Piers was aware of a change in the public's perception of him, something he put down to his treatment of Susan Boyle. 'What propelled me to worldwide fame is largely Susan Boyle,' he admitted. 'I have been passionate about my duty of care towards her and I think that has changed attitudes towards me, but I feel adamant that the maelstrom resulting from this year's *BGT* finale was hugely overplayed. Susan Boyle will especially become the standard-bearer for the response to the criticism of Simon Cowell and the way he does his business. She's not some weirdo; most people in show business are a bit eccentric, if you think about it – it doesn't mean they're not great talents. When people hear her album, they are going to see that she is phenomenal.'

And he was still capable of not taking himself too seriously. Around this time, he appeared lounging in front of a fire in an advertisement for a Burger King cologne. The presenter appeared to be wearing nothing but a large medallion and a piece of velvet to preserve his modesty but later it turned out that a body double had been used. Piers himself remained unperturbed.

It had been one of his most successful years to date, but he rather generously continued to attribute a great deal of his achievements to Susan Boyle. 'The moment in the room had been pretty powerful, but it was the way the YouTube clip had been produced that was magical – it was little short of a mini, Oscar-winning movie – and it was that clip that turned Susan from another good contestant into someone very special,' he recalled in the *Observer*. 'It resonated around the world and everyone who watched it immediately fell in love with her. She was the ultimate underdog: you were willing her to do well and, when she did, you wanted to celebrate with her. You've got to remember the timing – the recession was at absolute rock bottom, people were feeling utterly miserable and along comes this woman with this extraordinary spirit just when everyone needed cheering up.'

It had indeed been a huge television moment, but Piers too had made huge strides forward and was now almost as famous in the US as he was back home in the UK. And he was right that there was a certain brazenness about his behaviour that somehow allowed him to get away with a great deal; if he was criticised for being brash, he would simply own up to it himself, before taking the mickey out of just how ludicrous he was being. Surely his status as a national treasure could not be far behind?

CHAPTER FIFTEEN
THE NEW LARRY KING

At the beginning of 2010, the rumours were confirmed: Piers and Celia were officially engaged. It had been clear that this was on the cards for some time and, with Piers long since divorced, he was free to marry again. Even Celia's father had come round to the idea.

But there was still a television career to be pursued and next up was filming the new series of *BGT*. Simon Cowell was ill and so Louis Walsh stepped in to cover for him; knowing just how to drum up viewing figures, he promptly took a swipe at Piers. 'He's a poor man's Cowell,' Louis jeered. 'He's absolutely desperate to be like him, he even acts like him. He knows nothing about music – he's just a journalist. He's never had a hit in the charts, so how can he judge music? I honestly can't believe how he gets away with it!'

Naturally, all this was like a red rag to a bull. 'Louis is a poor man's Jason Gardiner and that's about as bad a place as you can find yourself in the talent-judging business,' observed Piers. 'He is a giggling, fawning leprechaun whose critiques carry the weight of a two-ounce gherkin. It's like having a grandpa on the panel!'

Cowell, who was still suffering from the flu, wearily left his sickbed to return to work early. Even Amanda Holden hadn't been able to persuade Piers and Louis to make up and become friends.

At the same time, all Piers' shows continued to make headlines. The then Prime Minister Gordon Brown appeared on *Life Stories* and was moved to tears when talking about the death of his baby daughter, Jennifer Jane. (He also discussed how he had met his wife for the first time on a plane and answered in the negative when Piers cheekily asked if he'd joined the Mile High Club.) Next up was none other than Simon Cowell himself, who opened up for the first time about his girlfriend, Hollywood make-up artist Mezhgan Hussainy. 'She's very special – she could be the one,' he enthused.

Life Stories continued getting the stars to open up, with Joan Collins confessing to taking cocaine and Geri Halliwell owning up to an eating disorder.

Piers mused on his success: 'Asking Alistair Darling if he's good in bed was difficult, but I did it,' he proudly declared. 'The more shameless you are as an interviewer, the better the interview. I have no shame about asking anyone anything – but, then, I *am* shameless.'

'Things just happen to me,' he went on. 'I was at Naomi

Campbell's fashion show for Haiti, and Kate Moss kicked me as hard as she could and ran off. Freddie Flintoff went, "Fucking hell, mate – Kate Moss just lamped you one!"' Then again, it had been the *Mirror* who had published pictures of Moss apparently taking drugs – perhaps the connection was the reason for her mood.

Really, it was Piers' natural curiosity about other people that was standing him in such good stead. 'When I read books on holiday, it's always biographies,' he once revealed. 'I don't care if they're about Matisse, Margaret Thatcher or Jade Goody – I'm fascinated by people's lives. When I interview people, I think, what if Sharon Osbourne came into the pub, what would everyone want to know?' Then again, of triumphs such as the Nick Clegg story (Cleggover), he said, 'And there you go, that's his obituary headline. He didn't have to answer. I'm not sure it necessarily did him damage, although he might have had a conversation with Mrs Clegg when he got home.'

The main thing for Piers, of course, was that he'd got a good story.

Meanwhile, over at *BGT*, Piers and his fellow presenter Amanda Holden were next to have a backstage bust-up, although it seems more than likely that they were playing up to get publicity for the show.

'I'm not Amanda – I don't share her view that you should sell your wedding and tell all about your sex texts,' declared Piers. 'She'll do anything, though, if the cheque's big enough.'

'Piers would love to have his wedding in a magazine,' snapped Amanda in return, 'but, with his huge ego, he wouldn't be able to fit a photographer in the church at the same time.'

Amanda's real role, however, was to keep her larger-than-life fellow judges bound to reality. 'Piers and Simon never behave,' she declared. 'I'm there to rein them in. They still have their spats and waste time arguing. Simon is ruled by his head and by his wallet, and Piers is also very cerebral. Neither of them thinks with their heart – neither of them has one, to be honest! I add a bit of heart and emotion to the panel, but then Piers pisses me off because he steals my lines. Once, I leaned over to him and said, "Ooh, he looks like the guy from Hot Chocolate! He has all the moves." And because we go to him first, he said, "You look like the guy from Hot Chocolate, you have the moves." Then they come to me and I'm like, "Er...?" It's *so* annoying.'

Of course, reality TV has often been accused of making people think they can become stars overnight with no work involved, but Piers was adamant *BGT* was not like that. 'The culture of celebrity has become a problem,' he admitted at a charity event for Norwood, during which he was interviewed by media tycoon Richard Desmond. 'You don't mind someone being famous if it's based on real talent – that's why I like talent shows that encourage people to chase their dream but what I don't like is talent-less wastrels who appear on telly just for the sake of it.

I find *Big Brother* incredibly vacuous and it chips away at the mystique and magic of celebrities. The glamour of Marilyn Monroe was something to look up to and be excited by.'

In the same interview, Richard Desmond also questioned him about *Life Stories*. 'My favourite guest was Ronnie Corbett,' he said. 'He got up in the middle of the interview and walked over to the side of the stage and started a monologue, and it was like watching comedy history. But Geri Halliwell was quite tricky to interview; she was guarded and difficult, but that's not to say I didn't like her.

'I spoke to Susan Boyle the other day. She said, "Everyone keeps telling me I am cracking up. I am – but with happiness!" Susan practised singing for a very long time before she became famous and she deserves her success at forty-eight, so, while most young people think they can be famous overnight, the fact is it is very hard work.'

Then again, Piers was thrilled by his new lifestyle and was totally open about it, too. 'Where do I start?' he said. 'The freebies, upgrades, best tables in restaurants... I did a "real job" for twenty years, now I do a bit of judging and interviewing. People treat me differently because I'm a celebrity. I couldn't give a toss about intrusion; when I get chased by the paparazzi I chase them back – I *want* to be in the papers. At least I'm honest about it. I haven't got "Hugh Grant syndrome", chucking baked bean tins at photographers then smiling at them at my next movie premiere to promote my sorry little ass.'

Although this was said with a smile, Piers was also making a point about the people who'd been so quick to kick him when he was down. Now, his life was very much on the up; he'd won and he was enjoying every minute of his fame and who could blame him? As for all the fuss he made about how easy it had been, the fact was that he was still working extremely hard.

Not that everyone warmed to him, it seemed. 'One said recently: "There's no other word for him but 'wanker',," Piers once said. 'But a lot of people I know are wankers and I like them. My persona polarises people: half love me, half want to kill me. I don't think I am a wanker in real life. My "personality" probably is, yeah. I'd hate it if I was called a terrible father rather than a wanker. If I get stitched up in an interview, I'll come back and take my revenge. I'm not quiet but I am less inflammatory, less overtly self-confident. I am probably more sensitive than people think, more generous. You have to project supreme self-confidence as a tabloid editor, but underneath of course you have self-doubt and, after you are sacked, you are not sure what to do next: whether you'll be successful ever again or if you're a washed-up has-been. But I'm positive: I've got columns, my *GQ* interviews, TV shows… I'm easily pleased – give me a cricket match, a ticket to Arsenal, my kids, Celia, my family. My celebrity, celebrity itself, is ludicrous. I find it wonderfully preposterous and fabulously fun to milk for all it's worth.'

Meanwhile, *Life Stories* was not just attracting interest

in Britain, it was playing pretty well over in the US, too. Around this time, it was announced that the veteran television journalist Larry King was retiring and CNN needed someone to take his place. Of course, as a talent-show host, Piers was already famous across the pond but, over in the UK, he was also proving himself an accomplished interviewer, securing emotional admissions from his guests and even managing to pull in the then British Prime Minister. CNN could not fail to be impressed.

When the offer was made, with a reputed £5.5 million annual salary, Piers immediately agreed. It would mean leaving *BGT*, but how could he turn down an opportunity like that? He'd have a global audience of 300 million and he'd also get to keep the remainder of his UK television interests as well as *America's Got Talent*. At any rate, although *BGT* had now enjoyed four hugely successful runs, there's a knack in knowing when to leave the stage. To turn down a chance such as this would have been madness and so he promptly signed up.

With excellent timing, given his recent piece of good news, Piers and Celia Walden married at the end of June 2010. He was forty-five, she thirty-three. The event was a world away from the circles Piers now moved in; there were no celebrity guests at the simple ceremony in St Mary's Church, Swinbrook, Oxon, followed by a small reception at a nearby pub. Celia wore a simple white dress and a handmade daisy-chain headband; the one moment of flashiness involved the couple leaving the church in a Rolls. Piers had earlier stated that he wanted 'a small wedding, followed by a big, *big* party', which is certainly what he got, although guests suspected that Celia might have had something to do with the simplicity of the proceedings, too.

'I hate to admit it, but I'm absolutely thrilled for the two of them,' said Simon Cowell (who wasn't present on the day). 'Having met Celia, I have no idea how he managed to pull this one off!'

Of course, the 'big, *big*' party indeed followed and was held at Piers' country home in Newick, East Sussex. Amanda Holden, resplendent in a peacock dress, was present with husband Chris Hughes; so too were Emily Maitlis, Andrew Flintoff, Christine Bleakley and Frank Lampard. Sarah Brown (wife of the former Prime Minister) and Alastair Campbell were also there. Guests dined on hog roast, fish and chips, and kebabs. Although the hospitality was lavish, again it was not over the top.

And so Piers began his transatlantic life: married once more, but this time with a flourishing career to pursue on either side of the Atlantic. In August 2010, he travelled to the States to stand in for Regis Philbin, co-host of *LIVE! with Regis & Kelly* and stunned viewers with an act of generosity. Contestant Christina Novelli was taking part in a quiz to win a Caribbean holiday and she correctly answered the question that Kevin Kline's first film was *Sophie's Choice* but ran out of the allocated time and so lost the vacation.

'Wait a minute, can I just say something?' said Piers. 'I just got married, right? I am supposed to be a dream-crusher: I would like to be a dream-maker. Why don't I pay for you to go? I am not going to have three seconds ruin your dream; I am going to pay for you to go.'

'Is this happening?' asked co-host Kelly Ripa. 'I am going to kick in the sun-tan lotion!'

The cost to Piers in cash was $6,100 but, in terms of his reputation, it was inestimable.

Appropriately, as 2010 drew to a close, another guest on *Life Stories* was Susan Boyle. As usual, Piers soon drew his guest out, in this case talking about the disappointment she'd experienced in not winning *BGT* and her conviction that her good fortune was over before it had really begun. 'I was exhausted, I needed somewhere to go to recuperate,' Susan admitted. 'Everybody knows that I went to The Priory – it was very scary. I wasn't allowed to see a television or make a phone call, I just felt as though I'd been dumped. It was probably the most frightening experience I'd been through.'

There were also interviews with Elton John and Cheryl Cole.

But not only was Piers interviewing the A-list, he had now become an A-lister himself.

The future looks exceedingly bright, although Celia has decided to stay in London, where she has a career in journalism of her own, and Piers will commute. Given her relative youth, a second family looks likely but Piers stays closely in touch with the children from his first marriage, holidaying with them and seeing as much of them as he can.

Of course, it's a long way from those dark days after he left the *Mirror*, when his career seemed all but over. However, it is the happiness in his personal life that seems to have affected him the most. 'If you have the right relationship, it doesn't matter what job you do,' he remarked shortly after he got engaged. 'I met Celia at a journalism event. I made a speech and died on my backside; she was the only person laughing. I talked to her – I thought, I like you. We complement each other: I've got a harder news edge, she has a literary head; it's a useful mix. I knew Celia was the one because she makes me laugh, hates sci-fi films as much as I do, takes ten minutes to get ready, writes better than me and looks like Brigitte Bardot.'

And as for the long-distance relationship: 'She comes shopping to Miami, Seattle, New York,' Piers had said before they got married. 'What girl is not going to love weekend trips to these places? She knows which side her bread is buttered! I'd have no objection to having kids with her. Pablo Picasso was still banging them out when he was eighty-six. I see bits of myself in my children: the youngest one is stubborn and determined to win; the middle one is a showman, the social organiser; the eldest has a fantastically advanced sense of humour, sarcasm and irony – he loves tormenting me.'

As for the future, Piers is unconcerned. 'TV's fake and

transient,' he declared. 'I won't be a famous TV star in twenty years' time – if tomorrow I had to go back to living in my Sussex village, I'd be quite happy. I've got a house there, nothing much changes – I love that. I know that Jeremy [his brother], my family and friends will still be down the pub, demanding I buy the first round!'

Then again, Larry King retired at the grand old age of seventy-seven, having enjoyed a successful career in television that lasted for over five decades. Piers Morgan might have some way to go, after all.